Kaukab:

REMARKABLE BEDOUIN WOMEN

By

Smadar Ben-Asher

Israel Academic Press
2024

Kawkab: Remarkable Bedouin Women
by Smadar Ben-Asher

English Translation from Hebrew original: Amy Erani

Published by ISRAEL ACADEMIC PRESS, New York
(A subsidiary of MultiEducator, Inc.)
177A East Main Street • New oRochelle, NY 10801
Email: info@Israelacademicpress.com

ISBN # 978-1-885881-86-1
© 2024 Israel Academic Press

Layout and Design: Amy Erani
Cover Photo Credit: Yusra Abu Kuf

Dedicated to Yoel
(1951-2004),
who illuminated my life
and entrusted us with the best of himself.

TABLE OF CONTENTS

By the star when it sets. Your companion has neither strayed nor is he deluded. Nor does he speak out of his desire. This is nothing but a revelation that is conveyed to him. *(Quran)*[1]

.

PREFACE

The Meandering Path of Childhood

A young girl wanders through the intricately laid paths of the kibbutz. With the arrival of Rosh Hashanah, everyone received new shoes, and before Passover, all were given sandals. Aside from this everyday footwear, each child possessed tall boots for hiking and waterproof boots for the rainy puddles. The girl's fair cheeks dotted with freckles are a testament to the harsh Negev sun. "Freckle-face" was the taunt her classmates used when they wished to tease her. Her short haircut, the unimpressive handiwork of the visiting barber who was compensated per head, did little to add glamour. Green lawns stretched between the kibbutz houses and walking on the pavements required nimble navigation to avoid the oscillating sprinklers. Eskimos recognize ninety shades of white, but we, the kibbutz children, discerned just as many shades of green, the color that framed our existence: the lawns we mustn't tread on, the bushes that bordered them, and the myriad of tree species planted up to the fence surrounding the kibbutz, beyond which the small hills began, with their wild grasses that immediately wilt at the onset of the first heatwave. The sun's rays, masterful painters of shifting hues, transformed the landscape's colors almost hourly from dawn till dusk, through the sweltering summer and into the

---

[1] *Quran,* Surat An-Najm, (53): 1-4.

winter — which begins at Hanukkah, ends at Purim, and fades before we've had the chance to properly greet it. Grey concrete paths, with a uniform pattern imprinted upon them, meandered between the uniformly designed homes. Flower gardens with multi-colored trailing branches, white daisies, and orange marigolds adorned their entrances, declaring the residents' diligence that didn't cease alongside their long work hours.

Everything was meticulously organized on the Kibbutz. Every detail, no matter how small, had its designated place and time: the opening hours of the general store, the shoemaker, the electrician's workshop, and the secretariat offices were all prominently displayed on the doors (which were usually locked). The community's work scheduler maintained endless, numbered "recruitment" lists for various tasks — from tending the orchard to loading poultry or cotton. Beyond the fixed six-day workweek, members were occasionally required to give more of themselves, dedicating additional days to labor at the expense of their "Sabbaths" – surrendering those cherished days off that were gradually becoming increasingly scarce, for the betterment of the greater good. A duty roster was pinned to the notice board at the entrance to the communal dining hall, listing the names of those assigned to the tasks of "set up" and "break down" for holiday festivities or weddings. Assignments for guard duty at the gate and night watch at the children's houses are listed separately. In addition to these rosters, there's a carpool list for vehicles departing early the following morning from the kibbutz to Tel Aviv, a table of those going on vacation or taking leave, and a register of those eagerly anticipating a move into a larger apartment, or seeking to travel abroad. These requests were relayed through notes placed in the mailboxes of those in charge, while important matters were communicated in letters to the secretary-general of the kibbutz.

I became lost amidst this rigid routine. I knew that on Tuesdays, the dining room served meat patties, and on Fridays, hot dogs. My day was punctuated by other indications of a daily rhythm, like the sound of heavy tractors rolling out at 5:30 AM to the fields, the wake-up call of the on-duty caregiver at 6:45 AM, "Good morning, children, time to rise and shine," and later on, lights out in the children's house at 8:30 PM in the evening. It was of paramount importance to be assigned to a fitting placement slot and not cause any trouble. My existence was cradled within these boundaries, and everything I desired lay in the world beyond the regimen.

The internal kibbutz road emerged from Gagarin Square, so named because its construction was completed around the time of the first manned space flight by Soviet cosmonaut Yuri Gagarin. This dramatic event occurred at a time when the kibbutz still harbored the conviction that the Soviet Union was the beacon for nations, and just a few years after the kibbutz children's Purim celebrations were canceled to mourn the death of Stalin. From this square, the road led to the large gate, which proudly displayed the kibbutz emblem, skillfully crafted by a local artisan. Come nightfall, the main gate was secured with chains and padlocks; in the morning, the entry was reopened for the procession of trucks. Some brought supplies to the kitchen ramp; others, loaded with feed for the chickens or fertilizer for the fields, turned left toward the chicken coops and barns. On the main road outside the kibbutz, the one linking the heart of the country to the Negev, cars passed by every few minutes. We, children, would sit and diligently record the names of these cars in meticulously organized charts, row by row, as training for future life conducted within the confines of the constant filling of empty slots in lists.

Beyond the road, which we dubbed "the main road," Rahat began. Today Rahat is a city; previously it was a small town, but at that time, it was a Bedouin settlement sprawling across the eastern hills. The precise order, structured organization, and neat demarcations set within the straight and curved lines never intersected. Rahat appeared as a collection of tents in various sizes and makeshift tin huts, whose construction was seemingly never complete. To the left, near the cemetery, stood the prominent house of Sheikh al-Huzayl, large, sturdy, and conspicuously prominent in the landscape. We were told that the Sheikh had thirty-two wives and approximately one hundred and twenty children. I couldn't grasp how one could count children "approximately." In my group on the kibbutz, the "Omerim," there were sixteen children, and when Reuven and Ayala joined, we numbered eighteen. We were never considered "approximately."

From within the tents, women occasionally emerged, with their infants clung closely to them. In the eyes of some women who gazed at us from the shelter of their tents, I thought I detected a glimmer of alarm. I couldn't link this trepidation to our group of children, donned in blue hats with oversized shoes, short clothes, and a canteen with its long strap diagonally crossing their small torsos. I wanted to believe they were merely shy. Yet, In contrast, the young girls met our eyes with smiles. Around us, a flurry of small children scampered about, darting in and out of the tents. The women shouted at the children in a language that was unintelligible to us, frequently exclaiming, "Ta'al hon!"[2] Gaunt dogs barked with fervor, likely attempting to chase away the strangers edging closer to their homes. Children our age rode donkeys to the school, housed in the distant huts east of the flour station, even though the school day had already begun an hour or two earlier. Only a few men were present there. One stepped outside, hurling stones at the barking dogs to drive them away, and then gestured broadly with his hand, inviting us to enter the expansive

---

[2] "Come here" in Arabic.

domain of the "Shig,"[3] where several elderly men were usually seated. The scent of campfires lingered in the air, mingling with the sweet aroma of the hash-laden cigarettes they rolled. Our tall shoes were coated in a thick layer of dust, which we later brushed off with the aid of a special brush upon our return to the children's house, just in time for lunch. Amid this disarray, I felt wholly consumed by curiosity, yet simultaneously, a part of me felt at ease. There in Rahat, among the haphazard jumble of tents and the scattered remnants of dismantled cars, there was nothing to damage. Any hint of the rigid confines of the kibbutz was left behind at its grand gate, and for a brief moment, I was free to absorb the varied colors, and sounds, along with the scents, and to relax in the presence of disorder that no one sought to alter.

Years passed before I returned to the vistas of my childhood. An aerial corridor now connects the community where I've built my home to the kibbutz where I began my life, with Rahat, the largest Bedouin city in Israel, nestled in the space between them. The home of Sheikh al-Huzayl now seems minuscule against the backdrop of the surrounding towering buildings, some rising two or three stories high. Where tents and shacks once stood, now garages, workshops, and small factories have sprouted everywhere. Storefronts line both sides of the road, with the narrow space between them and the bustling street crammed with crates of vegetables and fruits awaiting to be purchased by those who pass by. From afar, one can spot slender minarets of the mosques, their gleaming gilded domes shining, alongside expansive schools, the police station, and city hall. The local community center, seemingly plucked from a foreign architectural magazine, is adjacent to a substantial clinic serving as a front-line emergency facility. A road, notably uneven, cuts through the city, interspersed with roundabouts

---

[3] Shig — The section of the tent where the men of the family sit for long hours, conversing and passing the misbaha beads through their fingers. Women do not have access to this area.

every few hundred meters, all graced by either withered plants or discarded heaps of garbage strewn upon them.

This time, I approach Rahat from the East, not the West. The unfamiliarity profoundly strikes me. It's not the strangeness or difference of its neighborhoods that I find unsettling. Language poses no barrier – everyone speaks Hebrew fluently, the words rolling off their tongues with ease. However, the Bedouins' sense of identity has shifted from Israeli to Palestinian. A mix of nationalistic and racist undercurrents permeates the air, and its stinging breeze is impossible to ignore. A complex web of government policies, security confrontations, short-term wars, and home demolitions, alongside political and institutional violence — rends the delicate societal fabric shared by the Jewish majority and the Bedouin Arab minority. I return to Rahat and expand my acquaintance circle to Lakiya, Hura, Segev Shalom (Shaqeeb as-Salaam), and the unrecognized Bedouin villages in the Negev. The sober understanding that what disappears by day stirs in the evening offers little solace. I sense the unrest in the eyes of the youth and the absence of tolerance, respect, faith, and hope. Gone are the days of roaming in shorts, tall shoes, a hat, and a canteen slung diagonally across my upper body: innocence has ceded its place to an understanding that a shared life must be built on mutual respect, informed understanding of the other, recognition of differences, and a willingness to see beyond what is immediately visible.

Twenty years ago, in a unique program designed for training Bedouin at Ben-Gurion University, one of the students wrote on her exam booklet: *"I've written the answer to the question as you requested, but if I do what you've suggested – they will kill me."* This student's comment led to the initiation of research on the necessity to tailor the professional ethical code for educational advisors to align with the traditions of Bedouin society (Ben Asher, 2001). Gradually, I became attuned to the challenges Bedouin grandmothers faced in sharing their emotional distress (Ben Asher & Marei, 2012); the Bedouin mothers striving to protect their children amid the security threat of rockets launched from the Gaza border; the messages conveyed to women by men that the warning sirens are merely Israeli propaganda to be ignored (Ben Asher, 2016; Ben-Asher, 2016); and the Bedouin children caught in the throes of war, unable to grasp the gravity of the reality surrounding them. The resilience program devised by the Ministry of Education, intended to provide psychological support to assist them, is not at all adapted to their specific needs (Ben Asher, 2018).

For over three decades, my professional journey at Kaye Academic College of Education, Ben-Gurion University, and the Mandel Center for Leadership in the Negev has brought me into contact with Bedouin women. I learned to distinguish the Arab students from the North from the Bedouin students from the South. I witnessed their pallor, exhaustion, and near-collapse from fasting during Ramadan afternoons. My heart skipped a beat each time they frantically rushed in to report a student's indefinite absence due to a looming familial threat or a blood vendetta. To me, they were all students like any other, whom I expected to engage with scholarly articles and produce coherent academic papers. I came to recognize those who persevered until they achieved their goals and also to discern those attempting to sidestep difficulties, sometimes even offering payment for written assignments. As years turned into decades in the recurring cycle of academic terms, I transitioned from one semester and year to the next without stopping. Occasionally, a personal story would land on my desk, offering a window into a student's individual experiences. I reviewed these stories, provided feedback as needed, and returned the assignment. Nothing predicted the pause for introspection on the uniquely complex and multifaceted lives of the

Bedouin community members, a society not of harmonious contradictions, but of clashing and wounding fragments.

When exactly does a large ship pivot its bow to alter its course? The ship's captain, familiar with the sea's pathways, anticipates a change in azimuth, while the sleeping passengers awaken at dawn to new shores. I was not at the helm of my life's vessel, but rather a passenger, sailing through the daily routine on the predetermined course of someone training myself for the lengthy and intricate journey into academia, teaching, especially engaging in the field of educational psychology, with its array of diverse specializations and responsibilities. Yet, when I joined the staff at the Mandel Center for Leadership in the Negev, I elevated my sights to reexamine my core values and beliefs, delve into my professional identity, and specifically concentrate on the unique challenges of the Negev and its residents. With this perspective shift, I found myself facing a new horizon.

At first, the landscapes before me evoked the images etched into my memory from the kibbutz children's Tuesday outings, yet those scenes have been supplanted by a stinging reality that has evolved over time. As a child, I never heard the term "Nakba," intertwined with the independence of the State of Israel. We referred to the Bedouins simply as "our neighbors," while the designation "Palestinians" wasn't even part of their vocabulary. The protests against the military government concluded around the time I finished elementary school, and the demolition of unauthorized houses had not yet become widespread. I deeply yearned to revisit the comfort of a curiosity that requires no order, but it had slipped from my grasp.

Was it my role as a regional psychologist in the South, or perhaps my transition to the Mandel Center for Leadership Development in the Negev, that served as the catalyst for an active change in my relationship with the Bedouins in the Negev? I can't pinpoint this transformation to a single event, but rather an expanding awareness that began to crystallize within me, embracing the shared lives of all Negev residents, including the Bedouin community. I embarked on a journey of discovery, to reacquaint myself with the emotionally rich social and cultural world hidden beneath the time-honored tradition of hospitality. The challenge of not knowing Arabic was an obvious barrier, but surmountable compared to other obstacles. Above all, I wanted to hear directly from the Bedouins themselves. While interviewing the men proved challenging due to their cautiousness and suspicion, engaging with the women opened up a torrent of vibrant, pulsating stories of their experiences. Interacting with them as students and peers in leadership groups allowed me to synthesize nuanced insights and gather profound testimonies of their lives. Gradually, their narratives formed a rich tapestry, like the intricate, colorful carpets Bedouin women weave for their tents. Beyond their modest attire and compliance with patriarchal family norms, I was privy to their full lives, characterized by a subtle, almost invisible struggle for independence, education, personal growth, and recognition of their capabilities.

Sometimes, I question whether we are living in the same Negev desert. To me, the road that separates the Bedouin city from the kibbutz community, with its blooming, lush green plazas filled with stunning seasonal flowers and its expanses of playgrounds, a swimming pool, and sports courts — feels like a vast ocean. Crossing this road takes only a few minutes, yet I perceive merely the surface froth, concealing its depths below. Nevertheless, in their homes and mine, the same sun rises and sets, the oppressive heat of the khamsin[4] is felt by all. The wind heralds a reprieve, drought

---

[4] Khamsin — a dry, hot, sandy local wind affecting Egypt and the Levant.

returns, hands embrace a newborn, though the shadow of another war looms, love and hope flourish. Amid these complexities, there emerges a deeper understanding that womanhood is not just a gender category, but an essence of being. These shared experiences bridge the gaps between our disparate shells. They have attentively listened to my words at various stages; now it's my turn to listen to them.

> *It's difficult for two seashells to truly converse,*
> *Each is attuned to its own ocean's verse.*
> *Only the pearl diver or the curator of the old*
> *Can affirm without doubt: it's the same sea they hold.*
> (T. Carmi, 1994, "Attentiveness," p. 41)

"Bricolage" (Interdisciplinary) Ethnography: Handiwork of an Artisan

Each story shared by the Bedouin women is deeply personal and unique, as are my encounters with them, one-of-a-kind and beyond replication. The journey to Amal's home via a tumultuous dirt road, riddled with potholes and littered with boulders left by floods; our discussions in a diminutive room within a towering office building, behind a door guarded by Kawkab's husband to prevent any unfamiliar men from entering; Faiza's request to meet at my home; and the drives through uncharted villages and haphazardly developed town alleys – all these experiences compelled me to reconsider the conventional methods I had previously employed. Most Bedouin women refrain from answering calls from unknown numbers, and despite sending them my contact details via text, my calls often went unanswered. Arranging the first meeting with any of the interviewees was particularly challenging, demanding Bedouin-like patience, that necessitates an altogether different appreciation of time. Often, establishing a connection required relentless follow-up, with repeated requests conveyed through an intermediary who relayed reassuring messages regarding my intentions.

On one typical workday, a few spare minutes suddenly became available. My fingers almost dialed her number instinctively, trained by countless previous attempts. To my surprise, she answered. Her voice sounded tentative and slightly wary, but she agreed to a meeting without setting a specific time. Gazing through large glass windows, I observed Be'er Sheva enveloped in a dense, yellow haze. A Negev storm, carrying grains of Sahara Desert sand to this southern city of opportunities, shrouded everything in a thick, suffocating fog. I sensed an urgency that if I didn't seize the moment, the opportunity to meet the woman on the other end of the line might never materialize. "I'll be near the community center in thirty minutes," I told her, suggesting she could direct me to her home from there. I hoped the silence on the other end was one of surprise, rather than withdrawal. Eventually, she asked hesitantly, almost as if concerned for me, "In this weather?" An hour later, we were seated in her living room. Her brother, a young disabled man reliant on the pension his sister received as a widow from the Ministry of Defense, sat at one end of the sofa, observing us silently. Eventually, her brother relented and left us alone. On the wall, a television screen of grand proportions displayed the perpetual circular movement of white-clad pilgrims circling the Kaaba in Mecca. The broadcaster's recitation of Quranic verses resonated throughout the room, providing a steady ambient echo, and serving as a kind of background music.

Our conversation took place in an almost intimate setting. Abruptly, she excused herself and returned with a sizable plastic bag containing photographs from her wedding and honeymoon with her husband, who was tragically killed in a military accident shortly thereafter. For one hour, a shared reality emerged in that room between two women from distinct nationalities, ages, and educational backgrounds, united by a poignant separation from the man to whom their lives were intertwined. Na'ama Sabar Ben-Yehoshua (2016) refers to this phenomenon as a "double consciousness state" to describe the researcher's acute awareness of being both the observer and the observed, a dual awareness that shapes and simultaneously contributes to the creation of their shared reality.

The tension between the desire to delve into the essence and the necessity to convey findings in generalized scientific language, places qualitative research in a realm of inquiry, filled with reflection and uncertainty regarding the very possibility that these two distinct realms exist simultaneously. Sabar Ben-Yehoshua characterizes such research as "dual-tracked," it serves as scientific documentation, while concurrently offering the narrative of a once-in-a-lifetime, personal adventure. This type of research relies on data collected through methods anchored in theory but is based on a unique data-gathering journey that cannot be replicated. In the past, I was accustomed to filling in charts brimming with data, regressions, and asterisks marking significant differences, meant to exhilarate the researcher as though they had discovered precious treasures. Nowadays, I am not merely seeking the generalized dimensions; rather, I am in pursuit of the personal, individual, and singular experience, which ultimately constructs a person's perception of the world. What, then, is the distinction between narrative research and the realms of art and literature? Amia Lieblich (2010) reiterates two principles: adherence to research ethics and profound reflection on the relationship between the researcher and the subject or subjects researched. In the seemingly vast space between the scientific and the literary realms, a rich tapestry of "bricolage" (interdisciplinary) auto-ethnography is woven, blending the two into a vibrant patchwork quilt.

Ethnography is a research method that involves collecting data from the field within the context where the behavior occurs. The researcher observes the phenomenon under study from a holistic perspective, considering various variables as a participant-observer, even if not part of the culture itself (also see Bar-Shalom, 2011). Clifford Geertz (1983, 1984, 2008) pondered how to describe a cockfight on the island of Bali as a reflection of social orders. According to Geertz, a people's culture comprises rituals that embody unique meanings for the locals, and the cockfight serves as a kind of simulation of social structures, embodying societal rivalries and strategies for dealing with them. Geertz contends that the cockfight is the locals' unique way of "playing with fire without getting burned." The anthropological paradigm Geertz developed, "symbolic anthropology," explores how human societies construct meaning. Geertz believes that understanding a society's culture is not a philosophical argument or a solitary mental exercise, it necessitates a flexible research approach that gathers a comprehensive array of data using diverse tools. This naturalistic research employs various methodological practices, such as observations, interviews, and text analysis, along with the researcher's experience and impressions, thus poetically termed "patchwork method," or in its French nomenclature – bricolage research.[5]

Bricolage research offers a critical approach that integrates multiple perspectives, theories, and methodologies. According to Sabar Ben-Yehoshua (2016), bricolage writing is described as a

---

[5] The term "bricolage" is associated with the structuralist thought of anthropologist Claude Lévi-Strauss and denotes the action of a craftsman who integrates a multitude of materials. The result is a novel combination of elements taken from existing systems, creating an interdisciplinary tapestry of interwoven components whose collective significance transcends that of its individual parts.

"poetic endeavor" — akin to painting a picture that evolves to include narratives and interpretations. The researcher sees these accounts as a new creation, feels a responsibility to convey this vision to an audience. Much like art, such writing seamlessly fuses emotion with analysis, blending the universal with the personal and documenting intimate experiences through a dynamic interplay of stories. Analyzing narratives in such research merges a theoretical foundation with personal impressions, metaphors, and literary imagery, blurring the distinct boundaries between researcher and participants. This writing style, where the researcher steps into the field as an observer and weaves personal experiences into the analysis, is termed auto-ethnography. What does this resemble? It's like a soccer game lacking a linesman who raises the flag each time the ball crosses an imaginary boundary. The subjective insights collectively weave a new, rich fabric that portrays a broader panorama of knowledge, far exceeding the fragments of life and shards of reality before they were pieced together into a new collage.

Through the women's stories relayed in this book, I aim to reveal to readers the deep-seated richness and colorful diversity preserved in Bedouin tapestries. Crafted over many generations by young, unmarried women, as well as older women whose faces bear the marks of time — wrinkled, and sometimes adorned with blue tattooing, all of them bent over their embroidery, crafting stunning geometric patterns, captured in vibrant shades of pink and purple. Alongside unveiling the rich heritage, I also wish to expose the piercing pain woven into their stories. Although their accounts are deeply personal, these narratives harbor both visible and hidden threads of societal trends and transformations within the Bedouin community at large. They reflect a struggle for higher education for women and the stabilization of their marital status in a society where polygamy is increasingly prevalent; challenges of raising children in a rapidly evolving world that exposes them to dangers without the protections typical of traditional society; while they cope with love and separation, life crises, death, and mourning.

The Stranger in Research:
Understanding from Another World

> *How shall I impart to a tree the flavor of its own fruits?*
> *How shall I convey to the string the movement of the bow?*
> (Adonis, 2013, p. 115)

Through his lyrical words, the exiled Syrian poet residing in Paris, Adonis poses a question that has resonated with me as I documented the stories of Bedouin women and brought them to print. Their narratives are deeply rooted in the ancient traditions of Arab and Muslim culture and carefully preserved like the branches of a venerable tree. Is it possible to convey to those who create the music of the strings the intricacies of the bow's movement as it vibrates through the instrument? Can we discuss the social issues of the Bedouin society that emerged from these women's stories, not merely as artistic discourse, but with the objectivity required for scholarly research?

The use of a stranger as a methodological tool has long been integral to the work of anthropologists and cultural researchers. Researchers transitioning from one culture to another must grapple with their own foreignness to the subjects they study. The inquiry of Georg Simmel, a German sociologist and philosopher known for his phenomenological approach to sociology, marked by unconventional, non-linear methodologies and for writing from a deeply personal, subjective viewpoint, through which he engaged with the world on a micro-experiential level. Simmel's essay "The Stranger" (Exkurs über den Fremden), published in 1908, explores the unique vantage point of the stranger within the social fabric. It is the very alienation of the stranger that enables an overarching perspective that transcends the personal differences among group members. The outside researcher is physically close yet mentally distant, thus offering a refreshing perspective, in contrast to a researcher who comes from "inside" (Simmel, 1950). James Lance, who lived for many years in a village in northern Ghana, sought information about the indigenous people's lives during the colonial era. Lance quickly discovered that historical knowledge was intertwined with painful memories of conflicts related to the white stranger. The historical understanding was shaped by the colonial and post-colonial experiences of the villagers with Europeans. Locals were cautious about sharing knowledge with outsiders, feeling a duty to safeguard their community's secrets.

How, then, can an outside researcher, entangled in asymmetric power relations, reach an understanding of the reality? At times, when I attempted to learn from Bedouin men about the sensitive issues that women discussed with profound pain, they dismissed my inquiries as irrelevant or illegitimate. For instance, when I inquired about *"nisuei badal"* (marriage where a brother and sister are exchanged with another brother and sister pair), severely limiting a woman's freedom to choose her spouse, I was told these marriages are condemned in Islam and occurred only as a result of restrictions during the era of the military government, which lead to a scarcity of women. The men claimed that since 1967, with the opening of the gates to Gaza and the West Bank, the phenomenon has nearly disappeared. However, contrary to their assertions, the women described such marriages as a common occurrence (see Faiza's story). When it came to the traumatic experiences of women on their wedding nights, the men refused to comment at all. Furthermore, they expressed anger at me for merely raising the question.

Discussing sexual abuse in Bedouin society was deemed "'Eib" (forbidden), and revealing societal secrets was considered a betrayal of the community.

One effective method to address the challenge of comprehending reality as an outsider is through "insider research," meaning research conducted by someone from within the society being studied. Sarab Abu-Rabia-Queder, who examines the integration of Bedouin women into the labor market, writes in her book: "As a researcher, I perpetually wear both the native and the feminist hats" (Abu-Rabia-Queder, 2017, p. 7). Queder elaborates elsewhere in her book: "I, the researcher, a member of the society under study and a lecturer at Ben-Gurion University for years, am intimately familiar with the Bedouin population, particularly the women" (pp. 12-13).

The stories of Bedouin women shared with me often touched upon the pain and hurt stemming from a patriarchal society that prioritizes tradition and culture over the individual. Over the years, through my experiences in academia and in various training and therapeutic settings, I have learned that the distinctiveness and external perspective of the researcher, therapist, or professional instructor can also be advantageous. This is particularly evident in matters concerning the body and intimacy, where cultural laws and norms do not apply to one who comes from elsewhere. I recall a particular incident during one of the university courses, where counseling dialogue skills were taught. Would the women have shared a different life story with a researcher who was part of the Bedouin society? I believe that the worldview the women revealed to me reflects the reality of their lives, despite the social codes prevalent in Bedouin society which prefer that difficult matters remain internal and not exposed to outsiders. This aligns with the traditional Bedouin proverb: "It's better for pain to stay in the heart than to be revealed and cause shame."

The narrative is intended for the listener's ears in the unique encounter between interviewer and interviewee. Despite the methodological limitations mentioned, I hope that the respect I hold for the interviewees and the ethical and moral interest I find in their stories and their quiet, courageous struggles justify themselves and tip the balance in favor of my choice — to share their stories and the insights derived from them in the public domain, even if they may not be entirely complete.

Within the Tent of Women's Narratives

Each woman's narrative in this book begins with a brief description of how I came to meet her and how I learned to recognize and value her. This is my way of taking readers along on a journey to the time and place where these women entrusted me with their stories. The accounts vary in their level of detail: some were conveyed to me with hesitation, marked by insecurity about the chosen words, or the legitimacy of what was said; others were told in a manner as if a flood swept through the desert, carrying away everything in its path. Two of the women requested to meet a second time, feeling that their story had not yet been fully conveyed to me, or perhaps sensing that their accounts gained further depth and resonance each time they retell them.

All the conversations were conducted in Hebrew. Most of the women spoke clearly and understandably, sometimes using simple, everyday language. I was particularly troubled by the question of what was missing, what was absent from the women's stories, perhaps due to the transition between languages: for example, the whispered understandings in the school hallways, at weddings teeming with guests, as they pass by one another with arms full of colorful laundry, or as they escort their mother or an elderly family member to the doctor in the clinic — all these interactions unfold in the unique Arabic dialect of the Negev Bedouins. Hebrew is always a second language. In our conversations, they quoted the Prophet Muhammad and skillfully recited proverbs and folk sayings in a free translation. However, something of the deep, layered authenticity of their culture eluded the conversation with me. I felt the gap between spoken and written Hebrew. At times, I allowed myself to transcribe their stories in my own language, employing words steeped in the richness of someone nurtured on the knees of the masters of Hebrew language and literature. This decision was deliberate, aimed at delving into and conveying the experience to the readers in the vibrant, precise hues I experienced. I believe language is a tool to recognize, understand, and connect emotionally with the person sharing their memories, heart, and thoughts with you.

The book is titled "Kawkab" (meaning "star" in Arabic) after one of the women whose story is featured within. This is not her actual name but a pseudonym, as was given to all other participants. The name serves as a metaphor for her life—a shining star descending from lofty heights into a harsh reality and, miraculously, is not extinguished. Kawkab's story illustrates the heavy price Bedouin women may pay for their desire to acquire education and embrace lifestyles of gender equality (albeit only in relative terms), somewhat resembling those they encounter in Western culture. Kawkab is not the only star. For me, all these women shine in the vast galaxy that spans the expanse of the Negev, and their existence is unquestionable even if they are not seen publicly on stages under spotlights, a privilege in Bedouin tradition exclusively reserved for men alone.

This book is comprised of four chapters. The first three chapters chronicle the lives of seven Bedouin women, who strive to transform their immediate surroundings, aware that in their collective Bedouin society, every shift creates ripples that reach far beyond their immediate circles. These women are not official representatives or recognized leaders, because the formal establishment reserves leadership positions exclusively for men and has never chosen them for these roles. Instead, these women are leaders by virtue of their inherent inner strength, inspired by the resonant echo of their father's or mother's words that they hold in their hearts, and from the formidable resilience they have developed to turn the impossible into the inevitable.

All of these women are breaking through barriers that once seemed impenetrable. Like them, dozens of women traverse the vastness of the Negev, and many more will follow in the paths that these pioneers have already forged. All the women featured in this volume have blazed new trails, transforming the cultural and social fabric of Bedouin society in Israel.

The fourth chapter is a theoretical analysis that engages with the social issues highlighted in the women's stories. These issues serve as the warp threads robustly stretched over a loom alongside the weft threads — the personal narratives. Together, they interlace and complement each other. The unwavering belonging of these women to Bedouin society and their collective identity (as Muslims, Arabs, Bedouins, and women) has never been questioned, despite the challenging lives, obstacles, and their decisions to break through seemingly impassable barriers. These steadfast identities provide the strength they draw upon to fulfill their potential, regardless of where life takes them or where they choose to lead themselves.

The women whose stories are featured in this book welcomed me into their homes and hearts, sharing their successes, pains, hardships, disappointments, and great hopes. I preserved their stories almost in their entirety within the first three chapters. The reflective insights presented in the theoretical chapter at the end of the book were written to share with readers the theoretical knowledge that underpins the thoughts and insights that guide me.

The first chapter, titled: **"Stars in the Sky of Education,"** profiles three educated Bedouin women as they navigate a patriarchal world that obstructs women's access to academic careers. The first narrative features a young Bedouin woman recognized in an honors program for her bachelor's degree, who later completed her master's degree and then got married. As a married woman, she was forced to relinquish her freedom and live under constant supervision in the confined space of her husband's family home, to which she moved after her marriage. Between pregnancies and births, she continually fights for the right to work, even under restrictive conditions. The second narrative recounts the life story of a Bedouin woman who managed to fulfill her aspiration for higher education by negotiating agreements with the men in her family. She resolutely overcomes social and physical obstacles, including flash floods that cut off her encampment from the road where the school bus passes. The third narrative spotlights a young woman, the daughter of educated parents who decided to enroll her in Jewish schools. After completing high school, she finds herself alienated from the Bedouin world community to which she no longer feels connected, a community that imposes its laws on her and seeks to erase the impact of her educational experiences within Jewish society, along with the freedoms that profoundly influenced her.

The second chapter, titled: **"Growth from Loss and Bereavement,"** focuses on the personal tragedy of two young Bedouin women who lost their husbands while they were serving in Israel's security forces. Thrust into the spotlight by these events, these widows were exposed to formidable social forces of exclusion due to their husbands' deaths in the military. Although supervised by their familial and tribal communities, these women, with support from the Ministry of

Defense and rehabilitation workers, managed to forge new lives for themselves. They achieved economic and transportation independence, while facing down expectations from their communities to adhere to traditional family codes of "honor" and "shame." This chapter also echoes the stories of seven IDF widows whom I interviewed in a profound research study conducted between 2014 and 2016 (see, for example, Ben-Asher & Bokek-Cohen, 2017; Bokek-Cohen & Ben-Asher, 2018).

The third chapter, titled: **"Social Leadership in the Inner Courtyard,"** reserves place for a different type of leadership — one that is primarily conducted discreetly and modestly, behind closed doors, aimed at addressing serious social issues within Bedouin society. The stories of these women touch on the struggle against sexual assault in a society where the existence of such a phenomenon is often denied. Furthermore, if such an act is exposed, it often justifies either a forced marriage of the victim to the assailant or a so-called "honor killing" to cleanse the family's dishonor. The chapter opens with the remarkable story of a woman who diligently addresses this issue, by advancing therapeutic alternatives and intervention programs unknown within Bedouin society. Her esteemed status and the respect she commanded from those who know or have heard of her, along with her forceful personality dedicated to changing reality, even prompted the head of the local authority to acknowledge the existence of the phenomenon and the need to address it, even if he later withdraws to the safe territories of a traditional society that denies such issues.

The narratives of the women presented in the book culminate with the story of a grassroots initiative by a woman who deeply understands the plight of women on "Laylat al-Dukhla" (the night of consummation), also known as "the night of curses." Clad in her traditional garments, with a captivating smile and sharp wit, she guides brides and grooms into the night when they will first experience intimate contact between man and woman. She aspires for this encounter to be etched fondly in their memories as a blessing filled with gentleness, and not as a harsh conquest.

Throughout the book, I have concealed the identities of the women behind the stories. Much like the black veil that covers the faces of some desert women, I too was required to protect their identities fully and completely, disguising any detail that might reveal who they are. If anyone believes they recognized any of the women featured, I would promptly correct their misconception and remind them that in the vast expanse of the Negev, there are countless young women, any of whom could be the heroines of this book.

The fourth chapter, titled: **"Theoretical Study into Social Issues,"** centers on the conflict faced by Bedouin women who balance their traditional roles at home with working in the public sphere, despite the high personal costs of deviating from traditional boundaries. The discussion focuses on their changing social status, driven by community initiatives that address the challenges posed by outdated traditions incompatible with modern life. Additionally, the chapter discusses and presents the possibility of preserving the unique character of their culture while promoting social change that eliminates harmful and oppressive practices.

The book concludes with an **epilogue** that links the journey of the Bedouin women to my own, forming an affiliation built on an understanding that will forever remain incomplete.

Chapter I

Stars in the Sky of Erudition

Introduction: New Winds

In a world where shifting currents perpetually disrupt the established order of life, needless wars devastate cities and populated regions, and where refugees drift from their homes to countries where they will forever remain outsiders; amidst these fluctuating realms that are either crumbling or being rebuilt — it seems that today, the widespread recognition of the importance of higher education transcends nations and cultures. However, against this backdrop of broad consensus, a formidable barrier still obstructs women in conservative patriarchal societies from accessing higher education. "Perhaps I should have been born in the next century," mused one of the young women interviewed. She and other young Bedouin women were born at the end of the twentieth century in the earliest Bedouin towns, both recognized and unrecognized villages, a time when higher education was almost entirely out of women's reach. For them, no clock began to tick, even as the world entered the 21st century.

The stories of these young Bedouin women battling for their right to education resonated with me like the deep, reverberating sounds of a bellwether,[6] emitting sustained, prolonged sounds that shake the air around them. Today, I believe that through their perseverance and wisdom, these women are the catalysts of the greatest revolution within Bedouin society. They do not despair, despite the lack of basic conditions for learning — such as, when electricity works only intermittently and suddenly causes the small computer screens, purchased with the little money they managed to gather to go dark. They do not give up, despite the lengthy walk

---

6 Bellwether— The large bell placed around the neck of the lead sheep that guides the flock. Over time, the term "bellwether" has also come to denote a leader or an indicator of trends.

from their homes to the main road and the prolonged wait at unsheltered bus stops, marked solely by a lone pole indicating the stop. Still, these women do not relent despite the men — fathers, husbands, brothers, or other influential and controlling figures — who obstruct their path, and despite other women who attempt to dissuade them from breaking societal norms; they steadfastly pursue higher education, even with the looming fear they won't make it home before darkness falls. These women are courageous and determined, laser-focused on their goals, and prepared to stretch their capacities to the limit in order to fulfill their aspirations to learn.

Kawkab

Another Galaxy

Kawkab regularly attended her classes dressed in a traditional gown, embellished with stunningly embroidered crosses that stood out against the black fabric. She wore a black scarf that left only her delicate and beautiful face exposed. From the outset of her undergraduate studies, she was recognized as an outstanding student and enrolled in a special accelerated program, which challenged students with rigorous requirements, enabling them to complete their teaching certification and bachelor's degree in three years instead of four. Her Hebrew was as proficient as that of students for whom Hebrew was their mother tongue. Having graduated with a bachelor's degree in biology and meeting the stringent admission requirements for master's studies at the university bolstered and amplified her confidence in her abilities. Her subtle and intelligent humor lacked any cynicism or malice, and her quick responses to comments made in the classroom fostered a unique social bond among Jewish and Bedouin students, with their distinct attire being the only visible indicator distinguishing them.

Midway through her second year of master's studies, Kawkab shared that she was engaged. Her announcement prompted a burst of joyful cheers from her classmates, which preceded the flurry of questions directed at her: "Who is he?" "How did you meet him?" "Do you find him charming?" Kawkab's response seemed reserved and somewhat mechanical, "He's okay. I know his sisters; they are my friends. They are relatively free to do as they please, and they can even go to the big shopping center in Be'er Sheva." Kawkab's answer was almost swallowed up by the celebratory commotion around her. We quickly returned to the agenda as I urged the students to begin the lesson. However, a sense of discomfort stirred within me. I recognized the look typically seen in those about to be wed — the excitement, the anticipation, and above all, the joy of love. None of that was present here. Once again, I was struck by the illusion of understanding. It was not a barrier of language, culture, or different traditions. The young woman was physically present in the classroom and engaged in academic discourse and social interactions, yet it seemed to me as if she existed light years away, in another galaxy. She moves among us, understanding our language and adapting to our social environment, yet we are truly unfamiliar with the reality from which she came or to which she would eventually return.

Writing a thesis is a mandatory requirement of the degree programs, and I encourage the students to choose a topic that deeply resonates with them. The topics they select reveal a broad spectrum of enduring struggles that continue to impact their lives. Writing their research thesis allows for a fresh, comprehensive, and deep reflection from a standpoint of understanding, forgiveness, and consolation. For the first time, many of them confront the pain they have carried in their hearts for years: growing up as the daughter of a blind mother, a childhood overshadowed by an alcoholic father, having "temporary" siblings in foster care, migration, bereavement, and parenting a child with special needs. Kawkab chose to write about forbidden loves among young Bedouins. She insisted on exploring this topic despite the scarce academic literature available. Tears glistened in her eyes as she defended her choice. I realized that, even if I never discovered how the topic of her thesis was connected to her own life, her soul was deeply invested in it, in this well of profoundly deep waters. And with great care, she wished, once more, to lift the stone lying upon this well and peer into the darkness at its base. In her thesis proposal, Kawkab wrote:

> *In the lives of Bedouin daughters, love is fraught with danger, profoundly influenced by the pervasive sway of their society over both daughters and sons. Tradition constrains their emotions, forbidding them to love freely. They must suppress their emotions, because giving in to them could cost dearly, potentially leading to violence and honor-based killings.*

A faculty member who specializes in philosophy and culturally sensitive education took on the role of Kawkab's mentor. I trusted both of them and assumed that the secrecy, the threat, and the terror embedded in the experience behind choosing the topic would remain hidden, buried deep within.

Two weeks before her wedding, in the final days of June, the class held its end-of-semester graduation party. As the graduates began to coordinate the final technical details for the event, it became clear that Kawkab would not attend. Her fiancé, meaning, the man she was to marry in just two weeks, refused to allow her to leave home during the early evening hours. A spirited protest by her fellow students prompted her to promise that she would try to attend despite her fiancé's objection. I saw a warning light ignite in her eyes, yet she continued to believe in her power to act independently, make her own choices, and maintain her autonomy. She clung to the hope of fostering an egalitarian dialogue within the marital relationship she was about to enter.

Kawkab did indeed attend the party. She arrived flustered and angry, sharing that her brothers had intervened, reminding her fiancé that he would only have authority over her after another two weeks. One of her cousins accompanied her to the central station in Be'er Sheva and waited to escort her home after the party. "You've been traveling independently to your studies for seven years, what's changed?" her fellow students protested. "Now everything changes," she replied as if trying to convince herself, yet not fully believing her own words.

At the end of the summer, the graduates began to submit their final theses. I hadn't heard anything from Kawkab. The lecturer who oversaw her work reported that since the wedding, all contact with her had been cut off. I sent her an email trying to encourage her to complete her thesis but received no response. Someone who lives near her informed me that her husband does not allow her to leave the house and has severed all her means of communication, including her phone and email. A few months later, Kawkab managed to send a preliminary draft of her thesis. It contained almost no sources from academic literature, indicating she was unable to access the library or even the academic websites to a sufficient extent, those we generally advise students to use sparingly, as they do not provide reliably professional sources. Her grades were outstanding, and only needed to complete her thesis for us to confirm the completion of all her requirements and her eligibility for the degree.

One day, I answered a call from an unknown number. It was Kawkab's voice on the other end of the line, speaking rapidly and with palpable emotion: "I've borrowed the phone from my cousin who's visiting. My husband isn't home right now. I will finish the thesis, that's certain. My cousin will visit again next week and bring her laptop. I will write and send it." My attempt to continue the conversation didn't go well. I asked her if she needed any help, to which she responded that nothing could be done. I reached out to my colleague, social worker in the Bedouin sector, sharing my concerns and my desire to help Kawkab. Her response echoed Kawkab's own words: "There is nothing that can be done."

Another academic year drew to a close. One of the young Bedouin women studying at the college arrived at the program office and placed an envelope containing a folder with Kawkab's thesis draft. On the opening page, it stated:

In this work, I present various love stories of high school girls, none of which have happy endings. The majority of these relationships ended in violence, and one consequence of the love story was the girl's discontinuation of her high school education. There is a constant underlying fear of retribution and the potential of loss of life. In a traditional society like the Bedouin community, professionals cannot act or assist those young men and women who fall in love, because nobody wants to hear their opinions if they do not align with or contradict the prevailing traditions to which everyone is bound.

The thesis advisor and I reviewed the draft and sought to guide Kawkab on how to complete the work. This required a personal meeting, as is customary in the mentoring and defense process of a thesis. Kawkab disappeared again, and our attempts to contact her were futile. Three more months passed. Then again, unexpectedly, a call from an unknown number, and I could hear Kawkab's voice in the background. She promised she would attend the meeting. Her voice was weary yet determined. "I'm pregnant," she revealed, "I will finish writing the thesis before giving birth." I tried to attribute the heaviness in her voice to the advanced stages of her pregnancy, but I couldn't entirely convince myself.

Kawkab arrived for the meeting. The pregnancy was nearing its end, and considerable fatigue was visible with her every move. Layers of heavy makeup failed to conceal the blue bruises beneath her eyes. Although I am not a social worker who regularly encounters women who suffer from domestic violence, I recognized those marks as the imprint of fists. Her struggle to make it to the meeting was not merely verbal. Her eyes were dimmed. She awaited the birth of her child. The son to be born would bring honor to the father and perhaps calm him. He would see that she is a submissive and loyal wife. His parents support her. She would complete her degree and find employment. He would have to get used to her leaving the house and earning a living. For now, he was keeping her under close watch, forbidding her from going anywhere alone due to concerns about honor and shame. Her brothers had brought her here, and they were waiting for her downstairs in the parking lot to take her home. Her husband couldn't believe she only met with us. Even now, in her ninth month, he didn't trust her. He planned to take a day off work to make sure no other man was at the meeting, but his employer wouldn't allow it, so he insisted she not attend. Kawkab refused to cancel. There was chaos and violence, but she stood her ground. Eventually, her brothers promised to watch over her.

As the meeting drew to a close, Kawkab took command and outlined the plan of action: she would revise the work and find a way to send it to us. In about two weeks, she was due to give birth, and at the hospital, she would surely find another new mother who could momentarily lend her a phone. That way, she could call to inquire about her grade. Her melancholy smile upon saying goodbye was a stark contrast from the vibrant laughter of the exceptional student who had studied with us before her marriage.

Five years later, I reached out to Kawkab to arrange a meeting, eager to hear her story. She was employed as an educational consultant at a school in the Bedouin unrecognized villages in the Negev, not far from her home. Four months prior, she had given birth to a new baby girl. She agreed to come to the meeting with her infant and her husband, who would wait outside the room during our conversation, just keeping watch. The baby would be with us but wouldn't be a disturbance. She was comfortable with me recording the conversation — it didn't bother her. She was excited and looked forward to the meeting, enthusiastic for me to hear how things had worked out. She was wise and had learned when not to push too hard. Their relationship was stable, he trusted her a bit more now.

When she arrived for the meeting, I met her husband for the first time. I engaged him in conversation and inquired about his work. As we entered the room for the interview, Kawkab told me that the respect and attention I had shown him had a calming effect. He stepped out for an hour, but by the time we concluded our conversation, he was already waiting in the lobby. The stories Kawkab shared with me occasionally differed from what I knew and understood. I kept both narratives — hers and mine — side by side despite some discrepancies in the details. Even when we look at the same reality, we each perceive it differently, and the details of our stories merge into a distinct whole, each seeking consistency and meaning that we infuse through our individual perspectives.

KAWKAB'S STORY

Shining Star

I grew up in a large and bustling family. We are twelve siblings, and I am the fourth child. I have two older sisters and an older brother, followed by six younger brothers and two younger sisters. When I was little, my father married another woman. As far back as I can remember, he had this second wife. She has one son. I always say there are twelve of us kids, not counting him [Kawkab laughs]. Father was somewhat physically distant from us. True, we all lived on the same property, but he resided in a different house.

We lived in a remote unrecognized village, in the Bedouin unrecognized villages of the Negev. Until sixth grade, our home was a tent made from thick fabric, because we didn't even have a basic shack. Interestingly, we did have a solid house built from bricks until I was in second grade, but soldiers demolished our home because it stood in an unrecognized settlement. Subsequently, we returned to living in a tent. By the time I reached sixth grade, we were able to upgrade to a shack. It wasn't until I entered high school that we managed to build another house, which remains our family residence to this day. This is the sequence of my family's history — tent, shack, demolished house, and rebuilt home. One day, they photographed our entire area from above. By then, our house had been built, so it was spared from demolition. Whatever structures did not appear in the photo were torn down, and rebuilding was no longer an option.

When I was born, my father named me Kawkab. He told everyone that I was different and unique. Upon seeing me for the first time, he remarked that I was like a star shining brightly in the sky, blessed with exceptional fortune. That was his belief. To him, I was special, perhaps due to my fair complexion or perhaps because I grasped everything so quickly. While my father truly loved all his children, he loved me a bit more. Anything I asked for, he gave me.

From the moment I began my education, I understood that it could be abruptly withdrawn at any time. I saw this firsthand when my older sister's studies were suddenly stopped so she could stay at home and help our mother. She wept for days, but no one seemed to care about her tears. They claimed she would eventually get used to it, and eventually, she did. I was determined not to suffer the same fate. Ever since I was young, every time my father said he loved me, I immediately replied, "Just don't stop my education." It became a sort of game between us, but I knew it was my way of cementing in my father's mind that Kawkab would pursue her studies and would not give up. My sisters, both of them, only studied until the eighth grade and no further. In our family, there was a belief that girls who went to high school could be exposed to bad influences and might not remain loyal to the family. Despite this, my father agreed to allow me to attend high school. He told everyone that Kawkab is different.

The journey to high school was extremely challenging. There was no public transportation to school, so I walked forty-five minutes each way. I'm not even sure of the distance in kilometers because we would take shortcuts through the hills instead of walking along the longer dirt road. In the winter, I sometimes managed to get a ride to school, but that wasn't always possible, and at times I found myself walking in the rain. Despite all this, I never missed a day of school.

I graduated high school with honors and enrolled in a college program to study to become a biology teacher. Despite being quite reserved, I was somehow selected for the honors program, a selection process that remains a mystery to me. The commute to college was undoubtedly the most arduous part of this undertaking. The academic coursework and exams were not as difficult for me as the challenge posed by my daily travel to and from college. Each day, I walked forty-five minutes to the bus station and waited for a bus to Be'er Sheva. My journey on the bus would take an hour since it stopped at every station along the route. When I reached Be'er Sheva, I would transfer to another city bus that took another half-hour to reach the college. Sometimes, I would leave my house at six in the morning to ensure I arrived on time for my first class at nine.

When I completed my undergraduate degree, I was twenty-three, an age at which marriage is traditionally expected in our community. Nevertheless, I decided to continue my education. I enrolled in a master's program at Ben-Gurion University. Although I enjoyed my studies and excelled, my family was concerned because I was still unmarried. One man approached my family, expressing his desire to marry me. He was already married and wanted me as his second wife. I declined his proposal. Instead, I chose to pursue a master's degree in educational counseling at a college. My family believed that for Bedouin women, it was safer to study at a college rather than a university.

Once, I was at a big shopping center with my friends. One of them had car trouble, and she called her brother to pick her up. When he saw me, he told his sister, "I want her." My friend later revealed that her brother had already spoken about me several times. I knew his sisters — they were my friends and well-educated. Their parents allowed them to go shopping alone, so I thought they were part of a progressive and enlightened family, and that their brother would likely afford me a degree of independence. I also preferred to marry someone who was not already married. That's why I agreed to marry him.

In June, at the end of my second academic year, the graduation party was planned. Suddenly, he said, "Don't go to the party." We were still just engaged, not yet married. This raised concerns for me, but... I don't know... by that time, I felt like I didn't have much of a choice. I was twenty-six. He pursued me, and the other man who was interested in me was already married. I thought he was jealous, which was normal and acceptable. I never anticipated it would become difficult later on. I constantly reassured myself: his sisters are well-educated; each one drives her own car. Indeed, even now, his sisters drive themselves everywhere freely, and he never comments on their actions — only mine. And when I say to him, "Look, your sister Sarah goes shopping herself in Be'er Sheva," he responds, "Don't talk about Sarah. I am not her husband; I am your husband." In July, immediately after I completed my master's studies, I got married, with only my thesis left to complete. Somehow, I believed that I could be married and still retain some freedom in making my day-to-day life choices.

"It's Challenging for an Educated Woman to Live with a Bedouin Man."

The challenges I witnessed in my parents' lives did not prepare me for what I experienced with my husband. It appears that it is indeed difficult for an educated Bedouin woman to live with a Bedouin man. An educated woman must brace herself for numerous difficulties. I think this discord stems from our culture. From the first day we were married, he began to scrutinize everything I did. I distinctly remember the first time I wanted to check my email after getting married. He asked me, "What is an email?" After I explained it to him, he sat beside me at the computer and instructed, "Open all the emails you have for me to see." One of the messages was from one of my [male] cousins. He sent me a simple message: "I'm going to school tomorrow, how are you getting there?" That email triggered the first disturbance my husband caused. He deleted my cousin's number from my phone and decreed that I was no longer allowed to go to work. He confiscated my phone and computer and asserted, "Don't think that just because you're educated and employed, you're the man of the house." Before we got married, my father told him, "Kawkab is in the midst of her studies. You need to allow her to finish her degree, and perhaps she'll continue to further studies later on." My father may not know what a doctorate entails, but he recognized my desire and ambition to advance academically. My husband initially agreed to all these conditions, but ultimately, the reality turned out quite differently.

I left home and returned to my parents several times. On one occasion, we nearly divorced, but my husband refused to let me go. I told him that we were ending our life together, but he wasn't prepared to accept that. Eventually, I got past this decision. During a difficult period when he was unemployed, I suggested that I should return to work. Frustrated, I questioned how I — nearly holding a master's degree and with six years of teaching experience — could be confined to the house like women who hadn't even completed high school. My heart ached to think that after all my achievements in life, I would be relegated to just staying at home to raise children, without continuing to pursue a career or further studies.

I went to my parents and expressed my preference for a divorce. My brothers, my father, and my husband's father all sat down together. His father said, "I had no idea my son was preventing her from working." My father-in-law loves me and treats me like one of his own daughters. Ultimately, they reached an agreement and resolved: "Either she returns home with you and starts working, or she remains here with us." Only then did my husband agree to let me work.

I broke down numerous times, especially in the first year. The most difficult moments were when he took away my phone and computer. He wouldn't allow me to touch the phone. To this day, I am only allowed to use the computer when he returns home from work. He knows I reached out to my parents and told them everything, but such issues aren't seen as sufficient grounds for divorce. He controls me in ways he knows my parents find difficult to counter because they don't see these disagreements as valid reasons for divorce. For instance, if he now tells my parents, "I don't want her going to college alone," they would simply respond, "Well, fine, then take her to college yourself." I don't need a constant chaperone! That's how I feel. He denies me any freedom. He won't even allow me to think independently. When I sit in a room, lost in thought, he interrupts and asks, "What are you thinking about?" He even interferes in my thoughts.

Red Lines

Things are better now than they used to be. It's not the life I envisioned, but it's an improvement. I've adapted. I live with it. We've been together for about five and a half years. We've started to understand each other. I know exactly where his sensitivities lie, and I steer clear of them. He has his red lines. For instance, when there are school trips that involve both male and female teachers traveling together, I do not participate. I'm not even permitted to travel with my parents or his sisters; I'm not allowed to go out with anyone else except him. This is difficult for me, very difficult.

After our children were born, the situation began to gradually improve. He saw me as more involved with the children and the family, which eased his fears that I might leave him for someone more educated. He had only finished high school and was an average student without even receiving a Teudat Bagrut[7]. I don't seek the kind of freedom Jewish girls have, where they can even live with their boyfriends before marriage. I desire freedom within the constraints of Bedouin culture. I seek security and a sense of safety. I want him to trust me. I want him to judge me based on who I am. I've been married to him for five and a half years, and he knows me well. I have two children. I yearn for some distance from him, but that's not possible. He is with me all the time. Today, you invited me for a meeting because you want to hear from me alone. He took the day off to accompany me here, but I just wished he had stayed at his job.

I didn't ask him to stay home with the kids while I attended this meeting—I would handle arrangements for the children on my own, (although even in our Bedouin community, there are men who care for the children when their wives are out). I don't

---

[7] Teudat Bagrut— A certificate which attests that a student has successfully passed Israel's high school matriculation examinations. Earning a Teudat Bagrut is a prerequisite for higher education in Israel.

expect him to reach that standard. I simply wish to feel that he trusts me enough to travel and return home by myself. Today, I wanted to discuss our daughter's daycare fees with the community center director, but my husband wouldn't let me meet with the director alone. He insisted on being there as if he needed to guard me at all times. I wouldn't mind his joining out of concern for our daughter's welfare, or because he wants us to pay less, but I know he's there to ensure I don't sit with another man without him present. I long for freedom. When I gave birth to our youngest daughter, he was with me in the hospital for three days. I just wanted some space, some air to breathe. Other new mothers had visitors too, but then they were left alone to enjoy some privacy in order to bond with their newborns.

When there's a professional development seminar in Be'er Sheva for educational advisors or biology coordinators, he drives me to the seminar site and waits sometimes up to four hours until I finish, and then drives me home. That's our routine, to this day. Before each seminar, I inform him of the date and details. He either requests time off from work or adjusts his schedule to be free that morning. In his mind, he seems to fear I might fall for someone else, meet someone new. His suspicions aren't directed only at me — he distrusts everyone. Recently, he's shown a bit more trust towards me, but he still does not trust me entirely. He won't allow me to go out alone. I try to understand him and his behavior. Perhaps there was a past incident he hasn't shared with me. I sense he's hiding something from me. Perhaps his apprehension stems from believing that I've surpassed him — because of my salary, my education, my social status, and my job. He constantly feels as if I'm somehow better than him. Among Bedouin men, this is a problem; they want to be the most esteemed in the household.

I would like to pursue further studies, but he won't allow me to progress. Last year, I enrolled in a thesis-track program at Bar-Ilan University, potentially leading to a PhD. My husband told me, "If you're going to Bar-Ilan, tell me which days you have classes. I'll take a day off, drive you there, and bring you back." Eventually, I canceled my registration because he wouldn't agree to let me continue my studies. Even with his supervision, he was opposed to my educational pursuits.

I was once part of an honors program. I had almost forgotten that fact — I forgot that I had been an outstanding achiever. Now, I want to advance beyond my master's degree. If I were to complete a PhD and wished to work at a college, he wouldn't allow it. I think if I were married to someone else, or if I was still living with my parents, I might have advanced further in my career by now. I've seen people far less capable than me of reaching heights I've been unable to achieve because of the restrictions my husband places on me. Now, somewhat jokingly, he tells our infant daughter, "Don't tell me you want a cellphone," or "Don't tell me you want a computer." But my daughter will get an education because I am her mother. It's not that he opposes education; he's against a woman going out alone. I can already envision him taking our daughter to school and picking her up, or perhaps allowing our son, Mahmoud, to take her instead. His problem is not with the education itself; it's with the freedom. He won't allow her much of it.

"Would I Have Chosen Differently?"

I often ask myself: If I had known beforehand what I know now about marriage, would my decision have been different? I was still unmarried at age twenty-six, considered somewhat late for women in our community to marry. My sisters were married by the age of twenty-two. There were men from our community who were interested in me, but because I am educated and aspired to work outside the village, they preferred to marry a simpler woman.

Being educated is often equated with having greater freedom. However, in fact, men fear that an educated woman would assert her rights, wanting to control everything. Perhaps this isn't true for all men, but it's certainly true for my husband. My brother's wife, who isn't educated, goes to Be'er Sheva alone and returns alone. When I was with my parents, I also went out and came back on my own. Not entirely alone — I would go with my husband's sister. But with my husband — everything is extreme. Even if I wanted to go out with his sister, who is also my friend, he would forbid it. There's a teacher at school with whom I've formed a strong bond, and we have a good rapport. She often says to me, "I want to invite you to share a meal, just you and me," but he won't permit me to go. He knows her well, he knows her husband, yet he won't allow it. He says, "If you want to eat at 'Big' (a large mall) or somewhere else, I have no problem. You, me, and the kids will go now, we'll eat together and return. You're not going out with anyone else."

Despite the issues I've mentioned, there are also positive aspects to our marriage. We have a shared drawer at home where we keep our salaries, both his and mine. When my husband goes out to buy something, he doesn't squander money; he only spends it on household necessities. Everything he does with our money benefits both of us. He isn't like other men. His time after work, he always spends at home. If he wants to go out, he calls me and says, "Get yourself and the kids ready, we're going out." Aside from that, we take trips together, even traveling abroad, which is unusual among the Bedouins. For my husband, being free means being with him. Do you understand? He has no problem with us going out, but it has to be together, always together. I find this behavior suffocating it does not suit me. Once, when we had just engaged, my father said to me,

"Kawkab, I think I made mistakes with your sisters' when I chose their husbands. But with you, I think I actually got it right. You wanted this man, and you are educated. I think you'll manage better in life than your sisters." He didn't anticipate that my education and awareness would indeed make our marriage more challenging.

Privacy, Autonomy, and Independence

Privacy, autonomy, and independence — what do these words even mean? It's almost laughable to think about it. What privacy? My husband even reads the messages my sisters send me. This life is so different from what I had at my parents' house. There, I had privacy; no one touched my phone, I would go out with friends. No one knew what was going on between me and my friends, nor did they care. But with my husband, it's different. He lets me search his phone and know where he is going. He's not like the Bedouin men who cheat on their wives. He never cheats. He isn't interested in other women, but he's too clingy. He always needs to know every little thing that happens with me, even when I'm not with him.

When I began working at a school, he embarrassed me terribly. One day, my husband called me repeatedly throughout the day, but I couldn't answer because I was in an intense meeting with all the school's educators. These meetings required my full attention. Moreover, was also inappropriate to answer calls. Because I didn't respond, he left his job and showed up to my school. It was a Monday, and I finished early on Mondays. I was just getting ready to leave and hadn't yet seen my phone, which was on silent mode in my bag. When my husband burst through the door, I was shocked to see him. I grabbed my bag and said nothing to him except to express my intense anger. We drove home separately, one car following the other. Upon reaching home, I began packing to leave for my parents' house — that was it for me. But he locked all the doors of the house and pleaded, "Calm down, I'm just worried about you…" He tried to reassure me that his actions stemmed from concern. He begged, "Please, don't go to your parents, I'm begging you, I apologize." I stayed home, and he promised to give me more freedom. An hour later, I received a message, and he immediately ran to respond to take the phone and read the new note. He has no reason to suspect me since I have never done anything wrong. I would expect him to recognize that I am an educated woman with two degrees and afford me the respect and freedom I deserve.

"I Continuously Hold onto the Words 'I', 'Me', and 'Mine' in My Mind"

My home is next to my mother-in-law's house. She picks up my son from kindergarten and takes care of him until I return from school. She's like a friend to me. We share everything that happens in our daily lives. Initially, it felt odd, but now I've adapted to his family, and they've gotten used to me. At the beginning of our life together, he requested that whatever private matters happen between us at home should not reach his parents — a condition I am fully willing to accept. I don't tell her anything about my husband; it wouldn't help anyway. I am very strong, I have an education, a good job, and a driver's license. Another woman in my place wouldn't have survived all I have endured. But paradoxically, it is my strength that doesn't sit well with him. He would prefer me to be weak.

My father faces challenges with my sisters and their husbands, helping them navigate through the challenges they encounter. I've decided not to further burden my family. They married me off and wished to see me happy. Although I am not entirely satisfied, I pretend to be, in order to protect my father's health. Sometimes, I visit my mother with tears staining my cheeks. When she asks me,

"What happened? I see you've been crying," I tell her I have a headache and hide the true cause of my tears. She already bears the weight of my family's issues. My parents expect that, because I am educated, I should be problem-free. True, there have been unresolved issues between my husband and me that reached my parents in the past, but now, I chose to not involve them any further in our matters.

I think we will have just one more child. The children overwhelm him because they create chaos. He says, "Enough with the kids." Now, he only wants more children because his parents tell him we need more sons. He wants to please them, but for himself, he feels it's enough. I wish our decisions could be ours alone, not influenced by the extended family. He always talks about "us" and "we." I want to use the words "I," "me," and "mine." Sometimes, we go to the doctor, and I say to the doctor, "I want to know the condition of our daughter." After we leave, he corrects me, "Why do you say, 'I want to know'? Say, 'We want to know.'" Another woman in my place might just stay home, raise the children, and do as her husband wishes. But I hold onto the words "I," "me," and "mine" in my mind. A married woman shouldn't have to give up these words, even if she is Bedouin.

Amal

Admissions Committee

She stood before me tall, clad in the traditional attire of married Bedouin women from the Bedouin unrecognized villages in the Negev, a long, thick, gray fabric dress devoid of any ornamentation, covering from her neck to the tips of her toes. In eloquent Hebrew, she attempted to explain why she was a suitable candidate for a master's degree in educational counseling. Confident in herself and her abilities, she spoke of the need to enhance education among Bedouin children in general, and particularly among students with special needs. Many years of sitting on master's degree admission committees — at universities, colleges, and medical schools — had sharpened my instincts to be skeptical of "good" stories prepared in advance that seemed too tailor-made for committee members. It was precisely the assertiveness with which she presented this case that aroused my skepticism. I flipped through the pages of her application and read — not yet age thirty, a kindergarten teacher in the unrecognized villages, mother of four, with two years of teaching experience. As someone committed to the admission criteria for educational counseling, which requires three years of certified teaching experience, I wrote the decision on the front of the form — "Rejected".

A year or two later, I noticed she had applied again. In my capacity as program director, I consulted with my team members who had met with Amal to gather their impressions of the meeting. They hadn't formed a definitive opinion yet, but they shared how she spoke about the struggles of Bedouin women to break into education, a patriarchal society that hindered their efforts, and her persistent desire to continue learning. They suggested that she enroll in the "Teaching and Learning" track, which was better suited for educational and social leadership. At the top of the page, I wrote: "Hold." This designation, "Hold" signifies an intermediate status allowing decision-makers not to make an immediate decision and reconsider her acceptance at a later date. The process of selection and admission is influenced by myriad factors, and our ability to accurately select the ideal candidates has never been definitively proven. Time and again, I have faced pointed questions in our staff meetings: How could it be that a student who does not meet the stringent academic and practical fieldwork requirements of the program was nevertheless admitted? In contrast, other decisions that later proved correct seemed inherently obvious in hindsight. By the end of the summer, I reviewed the list of pending applicants. This time, I had to reach a decision. On Amal's form, I wrote, "Accepted".

In the course I teach for first-year students, I got to know Amal well. It seemed as though she diligently absorbed every word spoken in the classroom: attentive and meticulous, she even wrote the meanings of the words I used in her notebook. From student feedback, I know my language is sophisticated, and I speak quickly as if constantly fearing I won't have enough time to impart the elusive essence of the nuanced meanings revealed through counseling practice. My lessons are a challenge even the Jewish students whose mother tongue is Hebrew. Yet, I do not stop. Social sensitivity and respect for other cultures are deeply ingrained in me, in my lifestyle, and in my thoughts, but out of a responsibility to maintain rigorous academic and professional training standards, I do nothing to ease the burden for the group of Bedouin girls studying in my course.

Amal persevered. The quality of her submitted assignments showed marked improvement. I take note with admiration that Amal's achievements are on par with those of the Jewish students. I do not know how many hours of work it takes to produce an analysis of an experiment conducted in a lab with an advisor who highlights difficulties from behind a one-way mirror. I only receive the finished product via email, but I can imagine the moment she presses the "send" button — a moment filled with a blend of expectations and anxieties, hopes and memories of disappointments. Despite my repeated assertions that it is the work that is judged, not the learners, I sense that for her, the grade carries far more significance and deeper meaning than it does for other students, as it is tied to her self-esteem. Amal's profound inner motivation for education gives me pause..

Amal's Story

My Mom[8]

My mother was orphaned before she was a year and a half old. In the tent, divided into two by nothing more than a sheer curtain,

---

[8] In this section, where Amal describes her mother's life before her birth, I allowed myself permission to imaginatively fill in the missing details and took the liberty to craft a comprehensive picture from them.

three young girls and their very young father were left behind. Traditionally, a Bedouin man is not supposed to care for small children; that's women's work. He already knew that he would marry another woman who would bear him sons. In the meantime, with patience acquired during his childhood and adolescence spent enduring long hours sitting in the "Shig" (Bedouin hospitality tent), father gently combed the girls' hair, weaving it into delicate braids — skills nobody had taught him. His soul was moved by the sight of the little girls now experiencing a life disrupted prematurely by death; a life where the familiar rhythms and seasons they had known were upended. The eldest daughter was already seven, and the second sister was two years younger. In their colorful dresses, whose origins he did not know, the girls looked so small. They already knew how to boil water and pour tea into little cups. A spry boy would take the cups from them and distribute them to the men gathered in the hospitality tent. They knew how to look after their youngest sister, giving her a peeled orange and a pita just baked by their aunt in the courtyard on the Saj.[9]

A deep sorrow was reflected in the eyes of the older girls, but the youngest sister was playful, alert, and sharp-witted. She was gaunt and seemingly fearless. The father knew that none of his daughters would attend school. They were inseparable, and most of their day was spent on tasks from which most children their age would normally be exempt: folding blankets, stacking mattresses in the morning, washing dishes, and separating peas from their pods. Girls typically grew up under the tutelage of their mother and grandmother, who were expected to impart the family's rules, especially those concerning honor and attire. The eldest already

---

[9] Saj, a dome-shaped, black pan crafted from lightweight metal, designed to heat up quickly when placed above a fire, making it ideal for efficiently baking traditional bread.

knew she was required to rush to the tent and hide whenever a stranger approached. Her next younger sister mimicked her actions. The youngest, in contrast, would dash in and out of the tent. No one called her to immediately rush to the hiding area, and even if someone had, it's doubtful she would have heeded that call. She roamed around nearly naked, seemingly forgetful of what she was looking for, yet confident she would find it. When she darted out, she would fall over the tent stakes and stones that surrounded it, but she would immediately get up and continue to run. Falling on the hard ground was routine for her. Without glancing aside, she would keep running towards the destination she had set for herself. She likely never stopped because she already understood that no one would come to lift her and wash her delicate, scrapped knees.

The distant barking dogs wandering near the tent and bleating sheep gathered in the nearby pen typified their childhood soundscape. The scent of the campfire and the dust of the desert clung to everyone. Her father did not dwell on how, in the vast empty void, the fullness of existence had blossomed and instilled in a young girl the audacity to survive at all costs. He never asked himself where she found the courage to venture freely from the tent outward, exploring expansive new areas each day. This little one grew like a wildflower in a grazing field. They did not celebrate her birthdays, but her father remembered she was born in winter, shortly after the great flood. By the time she was four, the first son from the new wife, who came from the hills near Hebron, had been born. Subsequently, year after year, the second and third sons were born.

At the age of seven, the youngest girl cared for her little brothers, the sons of the woman who now reigned over the tent as though it were her kingdom. By age ten, she was already out with the sheep from dawn till dusk. By twelve, she was prepared for life, adept at preparing all the dishes that the women in nearby tents and shanties made for their large families. She knew that everything depended on her. The women around her also believed in luck. She thought 'luck' was a marvelous word, but also knew it was important to think carefully about how to help it find its way to their tent in the desert, far from any road. When she was nearly sixteen, her father arranged her marriage to his cousin Sulieman's son. She would be his first wife and felt that fortune had shined upon her. She was determined to aid good fortune with the same diligence and skill that she applied to her daily chores, which had become the rhythm of her life.

The small village she moved to lacked water and electricity, much like her previous home. However, the house was only seven kilometers from the road that led to the city everyone travelled to on Thursdays to shop in its bustling market. She had joined a large and well-respected family. Sulieman raised sheep and traded them, and she began to work alongside him. Despite her fragile and petite stature, she possessed strength, ingenuity, and astuteness for life. Over time, Sulieman married additional women, but she was the only one who worked with him as a team, in a full partnership that could never be undone.

That was my mother.

Worthy of Persistence

My mother gave birth to my older sister during the years the family wandered with the sheep, in search of pastures from one place to another. Her second pregnancy was slow to come. She traveled to Hebron to seek out the darwish (a saintly person or a Sufi Muslim known for his prayers and charms); to Khatib, writer of amulets; and to Attar, vendor of medicinal spices meant to aid waning fortune. Despite these efforts, the pregnancy and birth were delayed. A Bedouin man without sons is like a man without children. After five years of marriage and no additional pregnancies that might provide my father a son, he confided in my mother that his happiness was contingent upon his ability to father sons. She, of course, well understood that sons would expand the family lineage, while daughters would eventually join other families. He then informed my mother he had decided to marry another woman, a divorcee, and mother to three children from a Palestinian father. The thought of the strange woman entering her father's life occasionally crossed her mind. It's "Maktub" (fate), she told herself and continued with her usual routine, like someone who had learned early in life that even if she fell, there would be no one there to lift her up.

The Palestinian woman quickly bore him four sons. My mother did not despair and continued to believe that one day she would conceive. She had already stopped taking the concoctions brewed for her by the village elders and even ceased using the pills prescribed to her by the Jewish doctor who spoke Russian with the nurses at the large "Soroka" Hospital. Then, fortune once again smiled upon her. Thirteen years after their marriage, I was born, the second daughter to my mother and a sister to the sons of my father's second wife, two of whom were already attending school across the great wadi. When I was born, my mother named me "Amal," meaning hope. She said that if a person who suffers in life perseveres through life's hardships, in the end, they will ultimately receive what they deserve, as evidenced by my birth. Two years later, my mother had another daughter. She never brought any sons into the world.

My father's marriage to his second wife was not successful, prompting him to marry a third woman. Altogether, from these three women, he fathered eight sons and eight daughters. Many years later, he took a fourth wife, but I'll talk more about that later. So, I grew up as the middle daughter in my mother's smaller household, alongside my two sisters. During this time, I had numerous brothers and sisters in our polygamous family. As a child, I was different from the other girls in our family. I was constantly compared to my sisters, never to the boys, as daughters were considered inferior in their eyes. My mother, however, held a different view — she believed I was smart and destined to achieve great things.

My family is known for steadfastly upholding its honor, at all costs, particularly in matters of preserving modesty and dignity. Everyone watches over everyone else. We are not one of the modern families or a family who lives in the city of Rahat, where women go out alone to the market or the medical clinic. In our family, women must dress modestly, refrain from speaking with men outside the immediate family circle, or meet with strangers. Women are expected to work at home, remain in the background, and obey the men, who are the decision-makers and authority figures. My mother harbored ambitious dreams for me. Of all the wives, she was the only one who helped my father earn a living, which is why she would say to me, "I don't want the money I earned with your father through our hard work to only benefit his sons. I want you to fulfill my dream —pursue an education and establish a career." From the moment I was born, she instilled in me the necessity, even the obligation, to learn, advance, and become a person of significance and influence. This expectation was directed solely at me. My older sister never attended school because when she was seven, our family still wandered from place to place. My younger sister continued her studies until the end of high school, but she was a weak student who struggled academically. Today, she works as an assistant in a kindergarten, but her thinking is limited. Deep in my heart, I always knew that my path in life was through education; education would be my ladder to success. It's daunting to climb an unstable ladder that others are shaking, wanting you to fall, but I resolved to reach the top rung, even if don't know what can be seen from above.

Along the Way

We earned our living by raising sheep and selling them. In order to nurture sheep, we needed to continuously seek out lush grazing pastures and reliable sources of water. During my childhood, every spring, the whole family would migrate to distant grazing lands, returning to our permanent home in the winter. We roamed across the Negev, each time pitching our tent near fields that offered both abundant pasture and water. From the age of just four, my mother began to tell me that I needed to get an education: "Amal, look, if you don't pursue an education, you'll end up in the pasture. You'll spend your entire life with the sheep." Her words resonated deeply with me and had a profound impact. When I turned six, my mother was adamant that I must be enrolled in school, like the boys in our family, and begin my studies. She also decided that we would return to our permanent home and stop our nomadic lifestyle so that I could attend school. From the day I entered first grade, my parents stopped migrating from place to place, and my mother stayed at home.

In my initial school years, my mother was still unable to read or write. When I had homework, I would cry and plead with my brothers to help, but they refused. Seeing that no one was there to assist me, my mother was determined to do everything she could to ensure my success. In the small bag she took to the field where she watched over the sheep, not far from our home, she carried a single pita and a bottle of water. Tucked alongside them, wrapped in an old kitchen towel, was one of my textbooks and a workbook I had completed. The shepherd who worked alongside my mother could read. Day by day, slowly but surely, he would sit with her. The brown loess soil (i.e., predominantly silt-sized sediment that is formed by the accumulation of wind-blown dust,) served as their makeshift worktable after being cleared of sheep droppings, small stones, and thorns. My mother learned to read as though she were weaving words from the letters. At that time, I was already reading better than she was, but she stood by my side, insisting on hearing all the answers while her eyes followed the movements of the pencil that my fingers already knew how to guide to form the connected letters.

Our permanent home was a simple wooden shack situated in an unrecognized village. There was no running water, no electricity, and certainly no basic amenities like a medical clinic or educational facilities in our village. A single water pipe stretched for many kilometers from the town of Hura, a town officially recognized by the state. To access basic services, we had to walk to the main road, brave the relentless rain of the winter and the scorching heat of summer. The path to the road and the nearby school traversed the wadi that flooded every winter, with water rushing through in powerful currents, which disappeared after a few hours. The dirt road was riddled with deep potholes and crisscrossed with ruts that jostled any vehicle attempting to navigate them. Two kilometers from our home was a large dump for building materials and waste, where papers and fragments from construction bags were scattered in every direction.

The school was eight kilometers from our home. To ensure we arrived on time, we would depart at six-thirty in the morning. My brothers and I shared one donkey, taking turns riding it every three kilometers. One of us would ride while the others walked alongside. During winter, we often got stuck near the wadi — sometimes on the side closer to our home and sometimes on the school side — because the donkey would panic at the sight of the rushing water and refuse to continue. In such situations, we would wait for hours until the deluge calmed down before we could proceed. Sometimes, I would return home alone. Few people lived along the route, and for long stretches, I could walk without seeing anyone. I knew that if God forbid, something unfortunate was to happen to me, God alone could help me.

Elementary School

My first day in Grade 1 was terrifying. I felt as if I entered an alternate, alien world. I didn't know what a pen was or what a notebook looked like. Tears streamed down my face, as I felt I understood nothing. By the day's end, it seemed we hadn't learned anything at all. Our teacher sat by the board, and we all stared at her in fear. On the second day, the teachers changed, and we got a new homeroom teacher — fortunately, the new teacher was my cousin. Although I hadn't met her before, just knowing she was family comforted me and helped me adjust to the new environment. In Grade 2, we had a strict and rigorous substitute teacher. Once, I dared ask him if I could use the restroom. He seized the opportunity and said, "Read the passage on the board and then you may go." As I read, I trembled with fear. After I finished, I returned to my seat. The teacher then said, "Now you may go!" I asked him, "Where?" and he responded, "To the restroom." I was so overwhelmed by fear that I forgot I had asked to leave. To this day, I can still recall the words of the text he requested I read.

One morning in second grade, I told my mother that my school day ended after the fifth period, while my brothers finished after the seventh. My mother suggested I try walking home alone, encouraging me with, "You're old enough now." After classes, I left school feeling proud to be making the journey home by myself. I walked and walked, and after a mile and a half, I looked back to see one of my classmates and his relative chasing after me, throwing stones. Trapped, unable to return to school or continue home, I stood paralyzed with fear. Despite the blazing sun, they continued to relentlessly pelt me with stones. It is possible they were just violent, or perhaps they believed that a Bedouin girl should not walk alone anywhere, and if she did, she deserved punishment. After two hours, my brothers arrived and found me shattered and weeping. On another occasion, my brothers left their backpacks with me, instructing me to bring them home on the donkey. That day, someone untied the donkey, and it vanished. The weight of the three heavy backpacks I dragged home felt like the heaviest burden I've ever shouldered in my life.

From third grade onwards, we were taught by male teachers, in addition to female teachers. The male teachers treated us harshly and employed various punitive measures: they slapped us, struck our palms with iron rulers, and made us stand in the classroom corner next to the trash bin for over an hour. The math teacher would cunningly hide an iron ruler under his coat to strike us unexpectedly. In Hebrew lessons, the teacher would write stories on the board as soon as he entered the room. He filled the board, and we simply copied mindlessly, without even understanding what we were writing.

In fourth grade, we began to learn English. Throughout that year, we only sang the alphabet song and continued singing it until seventh grade. Apart from the alphabet, we learned nothing. In Hebrew, we knew a few simple words, and in Arabic, we just copied long texts from the Quran. I was a top student, and all my grades were a perfect 100, but we learned very little. Most of the time the teachers just spent training us to be obedient to them.

When I was ready to advance to eighth grade, my brother and cousin, who were beginning ninth grade, enrolled in the high school in the town of Hura. My father allowed me to transfer there with them because that high school also included a middle school division. I was delighted by the decision. My father said that my cousin (who is now my husband) would look after me, but he warned me not to speak to boys at school.

Arriving Safely at School

My studies in the middle school at Hura were a transformative experience in my life. Suddenly, I encountered intelligent students who truly understood mathematics and English, and who could read and write proficiently. I discovered that all the knowledge I had acquired until that point was merely basic, barely beyond what was expected at a third-grade level.

At the end of the first trimester, I received a report card with a grade average of 84. I considered that score a significant achievement for me. I was proud of my report card and the challenging journey I had undertaken to earn it. That day, my uncle came to the school to take his daughter and me home. He was the first to open and look at the report card. When we arrived at my house, he threw the report card at my mother and shouted, "Your daughter who desperately wants to be in the honors class? Look, look at this. She has an 84 grade point average. You might as well put the report card in a glass of water and drink it; it's worthless. Amal used to be an outstanding student, who earned perfect scores, but now she's a poor student."

During the second trimester, I didn't lift my eyes from the books. I skipped breaks at school and read late into the night in the large brightly lit room at home. I was determined to prove to everyone that I was capable of excelling in the honors class. My grades steadily improved, and I finished the second trimester with high marks. My family left me study in peace and no longer scrutinized any report card I brought home. Although, on the one hand, I had no support from those around me, on the other hand, I was relieved that they did not interfere. The truth was that I didn't need help; all I hoped for was that they wouldn't hold me back.

During that period, my father decided to marry his fourth wife. He built a house for her next to ours. She was a Palestinian woman who had endured a life of poverty, the death of her mother, and divorce from her first husband. She arrived at our home in utter despair. I obliged my parents' request to sleep at her place on nights when my father was not with her. Each wife had one night with him, and then he would move on to the next in a rotating schedule. My father believed this arrangement was best for all the wives, and he considered it fair. Consequently, I was forced to spend most of the week with her. She constantly shared her sufferings and past experiences with me. Her stories weighed heavily on me and painted a bleak picture of life. I began to harbor resentment towards my father for forcing me to live with her, I even dreamt of my father dying due to the rage I felt towards him. That woman adversely influenced my thoughts. I lost my ability to see anything good in the world, and I doubted that anyone would ever come to my aid. Fortunately, my father divorced her after one year, but it took me over two years to free myself from the negative thoughts and harmful feelings she had instilled in me.

In eleventh grade, we began taking the bagrut (matriculation) exams. Some of the examinations were scheduled during the winter, requiring me to return home after sunset. My brother, the second eldest, helped me by driving me home in the evening after the exams concluded. On one occasion, my father saw me returning late and asked where I had been. I told him I had taken the math matriculation exam. My father firmly told me, "Listen, you are not to take exams in the evenings anymore." Fortunately, that was the last exam I needed to take in the dark.

On the day of the first section of the history matriculation exam, the rain fell relentlessly from early morning. It's well known that we are effectively cut off from the world on rainy days, due to the flooded wadi. I needed to reach the school by two in the afternoon, to take the exam. All day, I stood at the window, crying. Tears streamed down my face alongside the raindrops on the windowsill. At one o'clock, I ran to my uncle, pleading with him to help me cross the wadi. Seeing me in tears, he agreed to drive me. I leaped for joy. I arrived just in time and passed the exam with a very good grade, which encouraged me not to give up.

The second portion of the history matriculation exam was administered in the summer. This test was also scheduled for the afternoon. I needed to walk to school, a journey of about an hour and a half on foot. Suddenly, I noticed numerous military vehicles patrolling near my village. I was frightened and unsure how I would get to school. The route to school required crossing over a very tall hill, from which it was possible to see all the way down to the road. My mother accompanied me there, stood at the highest point, and said, "Go, I'll stay here and watch you until you reach the road." When I arrived, I looked back. There she was, still standing in her black dress, out under the blazing sky, on that sweltering hot day. I completed the exam and made the hour-and-a-half journey, arriving home just as the sun was setting. The image of my mother standing at the top of the hill, vigilantly watching over me for more than an hour to ensure I safely arrived at school, is something I will never forget.

When I was in twelfth grade, my friends from Hura, who were daughters of educated people, began to plan what they would study and decide to which university or college they would apply. Each one shared her aspirations: "I want to be a nurse," or "I want to be a social worker." Later on, all of my classmates submitted their applications for higher education.

At the time, I had no concrete thoughts about what I wanted to be in the future. My only concern was how to convince my family to let me pursue higher education. I was certain that my father would not agree, and indeed, he opposed the idea of me continuing my education. By the time I finished twelfth grade, my father was already fifty-five years old. He had always tried to support our studies and provide for our large family, ensuring that his daughters completed high school. However, he believed that after high school, daughters should stay at home, and each awaits their destiny. He was particularly against his daughters pursuing academic studies because the university and college were far from our village, and students often returned home in the evening. He told me that ours was a respectable religious family, and in academia, girls might interact with men and not adhere to our community's rules. My elder brother, who had always supported my educational aspirations, left that year to study medicine in Romania. I felt as though I had lost my wings for seven years.

None of the girls from my area continued their education beyond high school. All of them finished twelfth grade and transitioned to married life. I couldn't sleep at night; my dream was to pursue higher education. I registered for the college entrance exam and told my father it was a necessary part of my matriculation exam requirements. Had I told him the truth, he would have prevented me from taking the exam. I successfully passed this exam as well. I had always been a trailblazer, but this time, I didn't know how I would manage to proceed.

Marriage: The Broken Promise

By the end of my twelfth-grade year, my family had already begun speaking with me about marriage. In May of that year, my cousin proposed to me. My brother, the next after the eldest, approached me and asked if I loved my cousin and wanted to marry him. I told him that I loved him but wanted to continue my studies. This was the first time I had openly spoken about my desire to study. My brother relayed to my cousin's family that I was postponing marriage for the sake of my education. My uncle, the father of the man who had proposed, responded to my brother (on behalf of his son) and agreed that I could continue studying, but on the condition that I would begin my studies only after getting married. This was wonderful news for me. I thought I was beginning to realize my dream and agreed to the marriage. The wedding took place immediately after my final matriculation exam. Up to that point, everything proceeded according to the agreement and the plan I had envisioned. Little did I know about the many obstacles I would have to face going forward.

A month after the wedding, I received a phone call from a friend urging me to immediately come to the school as the matriculation exam results had arrived. My husband was at work, so I quickly ran to my uncle and asked him to drive me to the school to pick up my diploma. My uncle hesitated and asked, "Does your husband agree?" I looked at him, puzzled, and asked, "Agree to what?" Then he said, "I'm not sure your husband agrees to you studying." His words pierced my heart like a knife. When I arrived at the school to collect my matriculation diploma, I discovered that I was among the top students in my entire class. I returned home feeling a mix of joy, sadness, anger, and tears. Even on this significant day when I received my matriculation exam results, they did not allow me to celebrate. A dark cloud hung over me.

My father-in-law broke all his promises. My husband worked with him in a large store and received a salary from him, but my father-in-law refused to pay for my tuition. He even threatened to withhold my husband's salary if I continued my studies. At that time, my father-in-law was not just wealthy, he was a millionaire who could have easily afforded the tuition for every Bedouin girl studying in the Negev. My husband had no influence over his father, who made all the decisions for us. In fact, my father-in-law decided for the entire family. My husband was only twenty years old, and his father informed him, "Your wife will not pursue further education. In our family, women do not study. She is solely to be a homemaker." My husband could not oppose him despite his trying to rebel. The power was in his father's hands. I left the home I shared with my husband

and returned to my parents' house, disheartened and also pregnant. My father said, "Amal, I have always been opposed to academic studies for women, but they promised you and let you down. And because I must uphold my daughter's honor, I am giving you two options: either you choose to live with your husband without studying, or you divorce him, and I will help you."

Hearing my father's response was incredibly painful for me. With a heavy heart, I chose to stay with my husband, whom I deeply loved. I tried to persuade him, pleading with every word possible. I involved other family members in our saga about the broken promise, but all to no avail. Finally, I said to my husband's father, "You deny me the opportunity to study, despite having promised me in the sight of God. May God hold you accountable for what you have done."

I understood this delay as a temporary concession for me to gather strength, before ultimately fulfilling my dreams. I gathered all my books and soaked them with tears. There wasn't a sad song to which I hadn't listened. Despite still being considered a bride, I wore only black clothes. I would sit with my husband, and my thoughts would wander as I sought a way to pursue my studies. I decided to save money independently and began working as a substitute teacher at a nearby school. I scrimped and saved all the money I could from my salary. I amassed all the money I could, even foregoing lunch meals. Meanwhile, my father-in-law continued to scrutinize us, always wanting to know what was happening inside our home. He would send his people to check what we were eating and what my husband was bringing home — often, my husband brought nothing, and there were times we would go without food. Unlike his other daughters, I didn't buy new clothes for the holidays, and my home was bare except for a few simple pieces of furniture. My father-in-law closely monitored us, determined to ensure that his son was not taking money from the store to invest in our household.

And then, just as I had predicted, God intervened to help me. God responded to my plea and punished my father-in-law for breaking the promise he made to me. He went bankrupt and lost more than three million shekels. Consequently, he was forced to close his store and dismiss my husband from his job — exactly as I had hoped.

At that same time, I gave birth to my first daughter, and we were in dire financial straits. We had nothing to eat at home. My father-in-law would sit with men from the family along with my father, pretending to care about us, though the truth was the complete opposite. Despite the hardship and poverty, I knew this situation worked in my favor. I did not tell my parents what was happening at home. After my daughter's birth, I approached my father while he was sitting with my father-in-law. I looked him in the eyes and said with all my strength, "This time, you will not tell my husband what to do, and I am going to study. I do not want a single shekel from you." Seeing he had no choice, he replied, "I will not speak against your studies to your husband. If you want to study, go study." I demanded that my father-in-law swear in front of my whole family vowing never to speak against my education to my husband. My father decided to remain neutral and not interfere, which felt like a blessing from God. This time, I was in a position of strength, supported by my brothers and father. I waited for my husband to come home from work to share the news. I could see the relief in his expression as if a heavy burden had been lifted from him. He said to me, "Tomorrow morning, you go register at the college and don't look back. I will help you."

The next morning, I stood at the gates of the college with all my documents in hand. I entered the registration office and enrolled. It was just one day before the registration deadline. There were no spots left in the elementary education program, only a few in early childhood education. Determined to study anything available, I was prepared to sign up for any open spot — the content mattered less than the opportunity to learn. A few days later, I was invited to meet the admissions committee. Two male professors and one female professor interviewed me. They pulled out my transcripts and began discussing among themselves, "Why did she choose this college? She should study something like medicine, at the least." One committee member turned to me and said, "You scored a hundred in every subject. Why do you want to study teaching?" I responded that I had no other choice. I will never forget their response: "We would be delighted to accept you."

College Studies

In order to study at the college, I had to leave home every morning at six-thirty. I needed to reach the main road in time to catch two buses. Before leaving, I would cook so that my husband would have food when he returned home at the end of the day. Sometimes, I found nothing to prepare. Every morning, my mother would give me a prepared sandwich and some fruit. My husband had just started a new job, and I didn't want to ask him for money. He would give me fifty shekels a month, and I had to make do with that sum of money. Fortunately, at college, I befriended another student who was as impoverished as myself. We would sit in a secluded room and eat. We didn't let anyone see what we were eating. The other girls in my program would go to purchase food at "Menza" (student dining hall). They all dressed beautifully and were accustomed to ordering a wide variety of food dishes. We had nothing and we felt embarrassed that we had no money.

On days designated for practical fieldwork, we were required to create crafts and activities for the kindergarten where we were training. At the end of the day, after all the other girls had finished their workshop assignments, we would salvage scraps from the trash and create beautiful projects. When they saw our creations, they would say, "Wow, what wonderful work you've done." I remember one day, as we were about to finish our fieldwork tenure at one of the kindergartens. My husband had given me twenty shekels in the morning, meant to last until the end of the month. When I arrived at college, one of the students approached me, and asked for money to buy a farewell gift for the kindergarten teacher and the students. I handed over the twenty shekels I had and was left with nothing for the rest of the month. On Fridays, I worked for a mentoring project, ("Perach"[10] — a national program for social impact), and I took substitute teaching positions during all the semester breaks. That's how I managed to save each year's tuition for the next. I felt proud to be the first woman from our village to pursue higher education and return with a diploma.

Throughout the first two years of my studies, I had one daughter. My mother took care of her and raised her. In my third year, I was pregnant with my second child, and by the end of that year, I had another daughter. During that year, we were required to gain experience in a school in a permanent settlement close to where I lived. As a fourth-year student, the principal asked the supervisor to assign me to their school system. He only had ten employment hours available for me. After working two days, I received an additional two days of scheduled hours as a "rotating kindergarten teacher," — spending each day at a different kindergarten. That year was incredibly challenging. I struggled trying to decide where I would be best able to prove myself: Was it in the school where I taught only ten hours, or in the other

---

10 PERACH, a national program for social impact, also means a "flower". PERACH pairs up needy children from underprivileged backgrounds with university students who act as their tutors.

kindergartens, where I rotated from one to another? There was nowhere I fully belonged, which weighed heavily on me. That year also marked the start of the second major battle of my life — the fight to obtain a driver's license.

Driver's License

The school where I taught was located a considerable walking distance from my home. Every day, I was compelled to walk an hour and a half each way. This was no easy feat, especially since I was pregnant again. I would finish work at 3:30 PM, and by the time I got home, it was already 5:00 PM. The winter days passed, followed by the intense heat of summer. My husband left for work at 5:00 AM and wouldn't return until the evening hours. I knew that if I mentioned getting a driver's license, everyone within my husband's family would oppose it. So, I decided to take driving lessons secretly, without telling any of them. I thought it best to first obtain the license and then deal with gaining their approval to drive. I asked my father for permission to learn to drive, as no woman in our village had ever driven before. My father heard my question, but did not respond. During this period, my elder brother returned from Romania and supported my pursuit of learning to drive.

I began my driving lessons surreptitiously, without my husband's family knowing. During the lessons, I wore a face covering to avoid being recognized. It took me a year and a half of lessons to finally pass the driving test, as I was constantly fearful that someone who knew me might see me at traffic lights. Throughout the lessons, I vigilantly looked left and right to ensure that no one familiar spotted me and reported back to my husband's family. After I passed the test and obtained my driver's license, I continued to kept it my achievement secret and didn't tell anyone in my family circle.

Then, I began to persuade my husband to buy me a car. It took nearly a year and a half to convince him, and when I finally did, I approached his father and declared my intention to purchase a vehicle. He responded angrily, "I'm upset with you. You went and learned to drive without telling me." This time, his opposition did not deter me. I asked my elder brother what to do. He told me, "Amal, don't wait for them to buy you a car. I will make the acquire it for you, and you will drive with pride." I gave my brother the money I had saved, and he purchased a car for me.

I remember the first time I drove the car; all the residents of our small village came outside to watch how I drive. They shouted various unpleasant remarks and waited for me to make a mistake — hoping I would hit something, suffer a flat tire, struggle to reverse and turn around, or even have a road accident or some other misfortune. I had to ignore them despite the great difficulty. I began driving to work, and suddenly everything fell into place much more smoothly. I continued my life with my husband, with great appreciation and respect for his stance towards me and my decisions, and the way he successfully navigated his family dynamics to enable me to realize my dreams.

"We No Longer Need the Entire Village's Approval."

During the third year of my undergraduate program, one of the lecturers announced that our college had launched a new master's program in educational counseling, in which we would be able to participate in the future. Her statement amused my classmates, who murmured among themselves, "We're barely finishing our B.A. degrees...how can she talk to us about an M.A.?" Nevertheless, the lecturer's words remained with me and continually echoed in my mind.

Having specialized in special needs education, I began working at a special needs school. The student population was challenging, made up of individuals with developmental delays and various other special needs. I worked there full-time and had two successful years, taking on several roles voluntarily. Despite the heavy workload, the principal supported me. He took pride in my achievements, valued my contributions, and continually reinforced my efforts. I felt I had overcome many obstacles in life, and each challenge strengthened me and propelled me forward. I had now become someone who no longer waited for external support or encouragement. I made significant strides in special education, where I successfully bridged between the wider community and children with special needs. Initially, the local community rejected these students and was reluctant to collaborate with the school on joint projects. I served as the coordinator of community projects at the school. Today, I receive weekly proposals for collaboration from various groups and mainstream schools. For me, it was an accomplishment to have carved out a place for those who had been marginalized in our society.

When the time came to apply for a master's degree in educational counseling at Kay College in Be'er Sheva, I completed all the forms, submitted my recommendations, and waited. In May, I was invited for an admissions interview, where the interviewer asked me why I had chosen to study educational counseling. I responded that my goal was to help students out of distress. She bluntly told me, "That's not it." She then looked at the year I completed my studies and stated, "You don't have three years of teaching experience." I corrected her, explaining that I had the required experience because I had worked as a teacher before I began my studies. Three days later, they called to inform me that I had not been accepted.

At the beginning of the third year of my employment, when I finally had enough experience to apply, I prepared the application forms, along with the recommendations. At that time, my two-year-old daughter fell ill, and we were unable to find a cure. I decided to postpone my studies for a master's degree until she recovered. In March, a week after I gave up on my studies, I traveled to the holiest site for Muslims — The Kaaba in Mecca. Before we entered the site where the sacred stone is located, our guide told us that anyone with a request for God could make it upon seeing the Kaaba. When I saw the sacred stone, I cried and prayed to God to help me fulfill my dream of pursuing a master's degree. This time, I no longer needed the approval of my husband's family.

Once again, I applied to the college's MA program for educational counseling and was invited for an interview. The interviewer asked me to tell her about myself. I shared with her all the challenges I face, the struggles of Bedouin women, and their fight against a male-dominated society. The interviewer suggested an alternative program called "Teaching and Learning," but this time, I did not back down. I remember that before my bachelor's degree, I had wanted to study in the elementary education program but had given up because there were no spots left. I decided that even if it took ten years and I had to interview repeatedly, I would only choose educational counseling. After the interview concluded, I felt that I had succeeded, but the response was that I was on a waiting list until the last week of August. Eventually, when I was finally accepted, the notification was lost in the mail. When I ultimately discovered that I had been admitted, I felt reinvigorated with new strength, feeling that every obstacle I overcame only fortified my resolve to keep pressing forward.

During my master's studies, I felt as though I had found myself; this was where I belonged. We were assigned articles, and I delved into them, discovering new worlds. Unlike many of my fellow students — Arab and Bedouin women — who would skip over new words they encountered without understanding them, I maintained a notebook where I wrote down every new word and its definition. I read all the articles and completed all the assignments, aiming once again to graduate with distinction. The two years of study were an experience only those who have gone through it could imagine. I met people from various cultures and suddenly saw things differently. It was not like studying in the Arab sector. Here, in the college, when you sit in a group, you find yourself next to a native-born Israeli student, beside a student whose parents emigrated from Russia, and beside her an Ethiopian student. Every two minutes, I felt I was learning something new.

I learned the customs of the Jewish female students, their accents, and new words. I noticed e-v-e-r-y-thing: how they behaved together, how they responded to one another, how they argued, and how they resolved conflicts. This was different, that was different, it was all different. I discovered that they operated independently in life, utterly indifferent to what others or even their families thought. Meanwhile, in everything I did, I awaited family approval. I told myself, "That's it, Amal, you no longer need the entire village's approvals." After two years, I felt like someone who had entered the ocean and shed all their heavy burdens, everything unnecessary, emerging cleansed and unburdened.

I adopted the good traits from my fellow students and applied them to my life and work. I can be a Bedouin woman, maintain honor and modesty, and also be an independent woman who makes her own life decisions. In my village, I was still viewed with criticism and harsh judgment. They always made me feel guilty for leaving the house in the morning and returning after dark, leaving my five children with my mother. They still think a woman's role is solely to be a homemaker.

In the second year of the MA degree, we had to choose a thesis topic. I wrote about additional Bedouin women who had broken barriers to pursue higher education. Each had a unique story, yet their narratives were similar in the challenges posed by Bedouin society. I received a rather high grade for my thesis, but truthfully, I wasn't satisfied; I wanted to finish with an even higher score. At that time, I didn't know that at the graduation ceremony, I would be called to the stage as one of the top four graduates of the program, and the college president would present me with my diploma.

Tel Aviv and My Unrecognized Village:
Not Yet the End of the Road

Another year passed, and my thesis was submitted to a national conference for outstanding master's degree projects. It was accepted, and I needed to present my research in Tel Aviv. I had never been to Tel Aviv before, and I had never traveled by train. One of the program's female lecturers accompanied me. All the way there, I told myself not to think about the train but to focus on the presentation. On the return trip, my traveling companion got confused about the directions at the train station. Suddenly, I felt all my Bedouin instincts kicking in — I knew how to navigate the space even though it was my first time there. Ultimately, I ended up guiding the lecturer to the correct place at the train station...

With self-reflection, I see that once again I cannot take things for granted. I've learned to question extensively, unafraid to consider change or explore new paths. I remain devout and traditional, yet I selectively incorporate aspects of my faith and tradition that align with my educational and professional work, discarding what does not fit. I am not abandoning my identity but rather reshaping it, seeking alternatives that help navigate the changes the Bedouin society must undergo. I am part of a community that preserves ancient customs while simultaneously encountering diverse, more modern cultures. In our society, there is almost no discussion about emotions. Sharing experiences, fears, worries, and difficulties is rare. In the past year, as a school counselor, I met with at-risk students, students from single-parent families, students with disciplinary problems, and those from families that discourage learning — families that suppress and block the aspirations and dreams of their children. I have seen female students battling societal pressures to avoid early marriages, women students suffering from the polygamy prevalent in the Bedouin community, as well as female students who have been sexually harassed or abused. My work as a counselor is challenging and deeply engaging. I feel that I am doing something meaningful that I will never regret. In my heart, I hear the voice of my mother who told me when I was young, "You won't remain with the sheep; you will do something good and significant."

I want to address sensitive issues, albeit delicately, in a way that does not cause me harm as a Bedouin woman. I know I need to expand my circle of collaborating partners as much as possible. Today, when someone speaks to me, I consider the matter several times from various perspectives. I think before I respond. I feel I owe nothing to anyone. I used to constantly take my family's opinion into account, always concerned about what they would say about me. Now, that is no longer the case. In truth, I do think about what they say or think, but they no longer hold as much influence over me as they did before.

Now, I find myself doing more things that align with my personal beliefs. Sometimes, the price I pay doesn't matter to me; what's most important is that I'm doing what I desire, following my convictions. Over the past two years, my children have also changed. They too have become more independent. I asked my eldest daughter, who is now nine, "What is your dream? What do you want to be in the future?" Her grades are outstanding. When I mention the idea of enrolling her in the school for gifted students, she questions me, "Why, Mom? It's easier for me here. Why do you want to take me to the most difficult place?" She wants an easy life, whereas I have always sought out challenges, relentlessly chasing after them. She's different from me. Perhaps once a path is forged, there's less need to hurry forward.

I invited my lecturer to visit my home. First, we toured the special education school where I work. I showed her my office, marked with a sign reading "School Counselor" alongside my name. She left her car in the school parking lot, and we drove to my house in my car. I drove confidently as if it were completely natural for a Bedouin woman to be behind the wheel. Two days earlier, it had rained, and the wadi had blocked the road. By now, the water had receded, but large stones swept along by the flood remained. My mother welcomed us and conversed briefly with my guest. I was surprised she was able to describe my life in her words — half in Arabic and half in Hebrew. Eventually, she grew tired and went back to tend to the children. I changed from my traditional dress into a simple, comfortable tracksuit. My lecturer had never seen me like this before. I showed her the small houses around us, homes my father had built for all his wives. She inquired whether we were concerned about the State potentially demolishing our homes. I confessed that such worries always linger in our hearts. The older children came back from school, and the eldest approached to say hello. We sat outside, basking in the lingering sunlight. The house was chilly because we didn't have heating. I shared with her my desire to pursue further education. She wasn't surprised; I believe she had faith in my ability to blaze new trails. We discussed the opportunities available to me. My mother watched us from inside the house. I feel that deep down, she knows and believes that it will indeed happen.

Adel

A Bedouin Student in a Jewish School

I first heard Adel's name before I met her. The counselors at the regional community high school she attended once told me at a professional meeting about a group of Bedouin students who were integrated into their school. They mentioned that all were outstanding students, and issues regarding their identities rarely arose. Not that they concealed their identities, but even their names subtly hinted at their desire to integrate: Emir, Hagar, Rafi, Yasmin, Adam, Adel, and Sraj. Notably, Sraj's Jewish friends called her Sarai, which she never corrected, objected to, nor took offense. The Bedouin parents of these students were all well-educated. They chose to send their children to the Jewish regional high school, believing it was the best way to provide them with a foundation that would enable them to study at prestigious academic institutions either in Israel or abroad. They respected and appreciated the school's teaching staff and never imposed any difficulties or made special demands. The students, including Adel, naturally blended into the diverse landscape of pupils who came to the high school from various places each morning. In their attire, as well, the Bedouin youngsters who studied at the Jewish school closely resembled their peers: colorful t-shirts, and pants lengths that varied from season to season. The girls wore their hair up and pulled back in a ponytail holder, exposing their youthful faces, with a distinct sense of purpose. The sole indication of an underlying identity-cultural conflict was the behavior of the Bedouin students during Ramadan. Some of these students developed a custom of "reverse fasting": at school, they declared they were fasting because they are Arab Muslims, while at home, they stated they were not fasting because they attended a Jewish school.

On another occasion, I heard about Adel from a young teacher in the Psychology track. She spoke of her with great admiration and said believed that of all her students, Adel was the best suited to pursue an academic career path in therapy or counseling. I attributed her fervent enthusiasm to the teacher's fiery hair color and her intense temperament. At the time, I had not yet recognized how truly visionary her perspective had been.

I first met Adel when she arrived as a student in my course on educational counseling at Ben-Gurion University. Her Hebrew flowed effortlessly, without the slightest hint of a foreign accent, a comfort reserved for those educated throughout their lives in Jewish educational institutions. Her curly black hair cascaded over her shoulders, defying the tradition that demands it be covered. Her face bore the fatigue characteristic of young mothers who are also students, already caring for infants. At that time, I was unaware that Adel was raising her two young sons alone, one of whom was a nursing infant born just a few months earlier.

Two years later, Adel returned to me as part of an academic research project she was conducting on the Bedouin boys and girls who had been educated at the Jewish regional school, nearly eight years after they had finished their high school education. By now, they were first-year medical residents, lawyers, physiotherapists, and speech

therapists, with some still pursuing advanced degrees. In terms
of education, their parents' choice of school had proven wise.
The high cost of this choice, however, was borne individually
by each of them, sometimes with a burden that seemed to
accrue endless interest. Adel's story was similar and intersected
in many ways with the stories of other female students Adel
herself had interviewed for her research.

Adel's Story

"Only Those Who Have Sat on the Fence Know How Much Pain Accumulates in the Body."

My name is Adel. I am a twenty-seven-year-old Israeli Bedouin
woman and a mother to two sons. My eldest is five years old, and my
youngest is two years and two months old. I live in Be'er Sheva, in
the Ramot neighborhood adjacent to the university. Those who meet
me can never guess that I am Bedouin. My father's family lives in the
settlement of Ar'ara, near Arad. His parents lived there even before
the State decided to establish the seven Bedouin towns. Back then,
the place was still called Aro'rer. The settlement is situated between
two roads — one leading to Dimona and the other to Arad. Apart
from those who live there, almost no one knows of the place,
although in recent years the town has grown and developed,
especially after wealthy contractors built huge villas there.

The grand houses everyone sees at the entrance to the town belie
the fact that most of the residents are extremely poor, and it is difficult
for women to find work outside the community. I love visiting my
extended family's home there, but I hardly know the other residents.

My father was born into a large family, and from a young age,
he was recognized as more intelligent than all his peers. When he

was in third grade, the school principal made a home visit to his parents and suggested he be sent to a better school in the "Triangle"[11] area. My grandmother, his mother, had no say in this decision. Now, as a mother myself, I can imagine how her heart must have shattered inside. In fourth grade, my father began attending school in Jatt (a large and developed Arab village in the center of the country). He lived with a local Bedouin family during the school term and returned home every other weekend. Picture a young boy traveling by bus from a collection point in the Triangle villages to Tel Aviv and then on to Be'er Sheva. This trip took three to four hours in each direction. When my grandfather, his father, met him at the central station, he would be worn out, hungry, looking lost and disheveled. During his weekends at home, he would nestle into his mother's embrace, clinging to her as though trying to capture and hold onto her warmth for the days he would spend far away from his family.

When my father finished high school, he was torn between studying medicine and engineering at the Technion in Haifa. His friends from high school in Jatt convinced him that as an engineer, he would earn more money and could help support the entire family. He began his studies at the Technion, captivated by the charms of physics and mathematics. He pursued a master's degree and a doctorate and returned to the Negev as a lecturer at Ben-Gurion University. He never made a lot of money, but he was highly respected within our large family. He met my mother while still in Haifa. She's an Arab woman from the North and is also well-educated. They married, and she moved with him to the Negev. My

---

11 The Triangle (Hebrew: *HaMeshulash*), is a concentration of Israeli Arab towns and villages adjacent to the Green Line, located in the eastern Sharon Plain among the Samarian and Haifa District. The eleven towns are home to approximately 250,000 Arab citizens of Israel, representing between 10-15% of Israel's Palestinian Arab population. (Wikipedia).

mother teaches English at a high school and is active in social non-profit organizations aimed at improving the status of Bedouin women. She does not hide her identity as an Arab woman from the North and makes no attempts to ingratiate herself with anyone.

My father wanted us to be raised as Bedouins, not as Arabs from the North. He desired for us to preserve our traditions and maintain a connection to his family. Despite his wish for us to be part of the Bedouin community, we began attending Jewish educational institutions. This was easy because our parents lived in a Jewish neighborhood near the university, making it natural for us to attend schools close to home. My parents collectively agreed that my brother and I needed to attend the high-quality schools because, in both their opinions, the Bedouin schools were not sufficiently challenging for us. I went to a Jewish kindergarten in Be'er Sheva and later, for two years, I attended a school in our neighborhood. I looked just like the other children, always had friends, and the teachers favored me because I was quiet and shy, and never caused any trouble.

When I was eight, my father suddenly panicked. Class parties began, and at one of them, the boys and girls entered the pool together at a private home. Suddenly, he informed my mother that the following year, my brother and I would be switching to the Bedouin school in Tel Sheva. And that's exactly what happened. For me, it felt like being exiled to a foreign land. I was very different from the other children. Yet, they did, however, seek my company, and I became somewhat of a class queen. I think this was due to my background. The local population was socio-economically weak, but I looked different and dressed differently. I could speak Arabic, but I struggled with reading and writing. My parents invested a lot of money in tutoring with a private teacher to help me close the gaps in my Arabic. I progressed quickly and soon became the top student in my class.

Despite my successful academic integration, that year was awful. There was violence everywhere. The girls were humiliated and always expected to yield to the boys. The worst part was when someone from one family had a conflict with a member of another family. Suddenly, the school was divided according to familial affiliations, while the hostility and disputes among families outside the school seeped inside. That year, the father of one of my classmates was murdered in a blood feud simply because he was known as an educated and respected man. I felt threatened. I feared that my own father, who was considered honorable in our tribe, might also be marked for murder in a family feud. My father didn't quarrel with anyone, but when someone is targeted, it doesn't really matter who they are, but rather how their death would impact the family's honor and who would mourn them the most. I couldn't understand who was vs. whom, or where I belonged. I practically stopped eating, lost a lot of weight, and suffered from both headaches and stomach pains.

At the end of third grade, the best thing in my life happened: my parents decided to transfer me to a kibbutz school. Suddenly, I had a sense of relief. I was no longer threatened. The children around me were much more similar to me than the Bedouin children in Tel Sheva. I studied there from grades four to six. Afterward, I moved with everyone to the regional high school for the kibbutz and moshav children, where I completed my high school education. I remember that throughout those years, it was important to my father that I excel; he was never satisfied with just average or good grades. He always wanted me to achieve exceptional marks, and over time, I embraced his desire too. I loved my studies, greatly admired my teachers, and received a certificate of excellence every year. To this day, I am immensely grateful to my parents for giving me the opportunity to study at those schools.

These schools were very special, both academically and in terms of the relationships between students and teachers. Much of my identity and who I am today is tied to those schools, but also to the fact that I might always sit on the fence and never truly belong to any one side. Only those who have sat on the fence know how much pain accumulates in the body from that position.

In ninth grade, I began to think about my future. I decided that I wanted to become a psychologist. From that point on, all my thoughts were directed towards this goal; it was my lifetime dream. At the end of tenth grade, we were asked to choose the majors we would intensively study for the matriculation exams. I chose to study psychology-sociology and also to enhance my Arabic. When I got home and asked my father to sign the choice form for the majors, he firmly opposed my selection and wanted me to study biology so I could go on to become a doctor. Those were very difficult days. I didn't want to be a doctor; I didn't like biology, and I felt a deeper connection to the realm of emotions and the mind. My father was adamantly opposed and refused to listen to me. I decided to sign the form myself and register for the majors I wanted, hoping that by the time I reached eleventh grade, I would be able to convince him. At the beginning of eleventh grade, I simply told him I had registered and pleaded with him not to be angry with me. He still did not like the idea and was extremely angry with me, but he understood that he couldn't force me to study something I had no interest in studying.

During that same period, we were told that the teacher who had previously taught psychology had left the school. I liked her and was deeply disappointed by her departure. Because of this sudden change, my class was combined with the twelfth grade section. I felt quite intimidated being with older students I didn't know. Then, a red-haired teacher entered the classroom, whom I will never forget. She loved psychology and cared deeply for us. Her classes were captivating.

When we had breaks from class, we would follow her like chicks freshly hatched from their shells, trailing behind the first moving thing they see. Sometimes, I thought we were fortunate that she was a woman because we loved her without fear or restriction. This teacher made me fall in love with psychology and, even more, inspired me to advance in the field. She motivated me to read more and more books, study diligently, and achieve excellent grades. She taught us that being a good person should always come first. We respected her, and our relationship was extraordinarily special. Looking back, I believe that this teacher had the most significant impact on who I am today, on my identity, my humanity, the educator I am now, and the educational counselor I will soon become.

Initially, we were just a few Arab students in the Jewish school, but over time, an increasing number of students joined, most from educated families whose parents refused to compromise on the educational standards of the high schools in Bedouin communities. I felt a sense of belonging with my Jewish peer group. Hebrew was the language I had spoken since childhood with everyone except my family at home. I felt connected to the culture of the other students at the school. I had almost no contact with my extended family, and I always felt like an "odd bird." At family events, I sensed everyone scrutinizing me, and only later did I understand that these looks were because my mother was "from the North" (considered snobbish) – different in appearance, culture, and mentality, and I, too, just like her, looked distinct. I graduated from high school with very good grades, but my psychometric score was not stellar. I asked my father's permission to study psychology either in central Israel or the North, possibly in Jordan, but he refused. It's not customary in our community for daughters to study far from home and live independently from their parents. My father was particularly strict when it came to his daughters. I think he always felt the need to prove to those around him that he was alright and that we were like everyone else — despite us not dressing like Bedouin girls; despite our education in Jewish schools; and our completely different mentality. Due to this rigid attitude, my father even objected to me working that year.

I turned eighteen and found myself alone. My school friends had either enlisted in the Army or volunteered for a community service year in their youth movements, and I had no other friends. I thought this was my chance to pause before taking on life-long commitments. At that time, my female relatives began getting married, but I still felt too young and unprepared for marriage. I decided to spend a year volunteering at a boarding school for children removed from their homes. My father vehemently opposed this decision, claiming it was a waste of time like no other, but I stood my ground. My mother worked for an organization that supported Bedouin women, alongside several men in influential roles. I asked them to speak to my father about the importance of a service year. Eventually, we reached a compromise that after my year working at the therapeutic boarding school, I would begin my studies.

Working with the young children removed from their homes was so difficult, it was as if all the world's suffering had been condensed inside that rented house behind the walls, into which they brought the social workers and the children. In that same year, I laughed and cried with the children, hugged them, and also forcefully intervened when they unleashed their pent-up anger on each other. The working conditions were incredibly tough, but the team of counselors and social workers was exceptionally dedicated. Together, we managed to cope, encourage, and support each other, while remaining resilient, without breaking down. Suddenly, I had a deep appreciation for the good, solid family I grew up in, despite my father's being so tough and stubborn.

The following year, I couldn't avoid it any longer, and at my father's insistence, I enrolled in a university for preparatory studies, so that upon completion, I could register for a degree in the field of my choosing. I disliked the university and had no desire to study in that preparatory program. Eventually, I discovered that it wasn't even the preparatory program I was supposed to attend. I left the program without explaining why to my father, and then during that time I wasn't in any academic framework at all. That year, I avoided my father as much as I could, and instead, I assisted my mother in her duties at the women's non-profit. I made every effort not to be at home when my father returned from work. He lectured in the afternoons and evenings, so during lunchtime, he would return home, and an hour later, he would head back to the university. I avoided meeting him so he wouldn't ask about my studies, and I wouldn't be forced to lie.

So, another year passed, and at its end, the truth was revealed. I remember my father was incredibly angry and gave me an ultimatum: either start to study, or get married. I was forced to enroll at Sapir College for a degree in social work. I interviewed there and also registered at the College of Teaching and Education. I told myself that whichever institution accepts me first — I'll study there. I was immediately accepted to the College of Teaching and Education and was awarded a full scholarship, due to my excellent scores on the matriculation exams. I waited for a response from Sapir College, and when I finally gave up on them and realized I wasn't accepted, I created a schedule for the teaching college and sent in the down payment fee. Then, on the first day of the academic year, Sapir College informed me that I was accepted. I decided to stay and study education, because I believed that perhaps God wanted me to pursue this direction.

I remember that in the second semester, when we started our practical fieldwork, I came home crying and told my mom that this wasn't my field of interest, and I couldn't study education anymore. I just felt like I didn't want to be a teacher, that it wasn't my destiny at all. My dream of becoming a psychologist hadn't changed, and I couldn't let it go. My mom advised me to finish the degree I had already started and said that afterward, I could study whatever I wanted. Her words calmed the storm raging inside me.

"It's Preferable for a Woman to Divorce Than to Endure Further Suffering."

At the end of the third (and final) year of my B.A. studies, I got married. He was a Bedouin from my father's family. I prefer not to discuss my marriage or its end. When I was pregnant with our second son, I encountered terrible conduct from my husband, behavior that deeply hurt me and contradicted the values on which I was raised. I separated from him, with an intelligent, opinionated, and stubborn four-year-old son, and a baby who had just been born. My self-esteem was very low, and my confidence in my judgment and decisions seemed to vanish. I decided to pursue studies in educational counseling — a profession that I felt was closest to psychology. Additionally, I felt the need to acquire tools to deal with my eldest son, who was deeply affected by the events of the previous few months.

I returned to my old room in my parent's house with my two young children. Under such circumstances, it's difficult to maintain a suitable daily routine for children. Life at my parents' house was tailored for adults. At eight o'clock, while I was putting the children to bed, guests were still arriving to visit with my parents, the TV was on, and everyone was roaming around, talking loudly.

Members of my extended family, both from my father's and mother's sides, did not view my decision to divorce favorably. They leveled harsh criticism at my mother who supported me. Yet, she did not relent, asserting that it's better for a woman to divorce than to continue to suffer. I could see my father was torn inside, caught between our cultural norms — which dictate that regardless of the issue, the woman needs to concede, and when she initiates a divorce, she's blamed for the situation — and his desire to support me. I didn't know whom my father talked to and what agreements were reached within the family. He resumed engaging in long discussions within his family's Shig in Ar'ara, returning home exhausted. His face was gray, solemn, and frowning.

My decision not to return to my husband was final. I couldn't envision a married life devoid of mutual trust, and that trust was broken. I believe that had I have been educated in a Bedouin school like the other girls in our extended family, I would have been less aware of my right to live as an independent and autonomous individual. I felt an urgent need to prove myself — to my parents, in general, and to my father, in particular — to show that I could cope alone without my husband, raise my sons without him, and also fulfill my other aspirations. Typically, in our culture, the sons belong to the father's family, so if a woman is widowed or divorces, the sons are supposed to remain with his family. This demand seemed utterly unreasonable and unsuitable for me. Even my mother supported my decision to keep the children with me. Fortunately, my husband relinquished custody of the children to avoid financial obligations. According to our religious laws, I still need to pay him back for the Mohar (bridal gift/purchase money), even though he's been living off me for four years. I was grateful for my good fortune that my parents lived in the city and not within the confines of their extended family, where everyone has something to say about everything. I decided that I needed to move forward for myself and my children and to prove to my surroundings that I am indeed strong and independent.

I experienced immense pressure from my extended family. It felt like they were trying to confine me to the role of the submissive woman, to accept my husband with all his flaws, and simply erase my own identity entirely. Just like when I was young and they sent me back to study at the Bedouin school, this time too, I felt the stark contrast between my society and what I believe and feel. But this time, I wasn't the "princess", or the queen of the class admired by everyone at the Bedouin school. This time I was a divorced woman, challenging the sacred norms of our society by firmly deciding not to continue living with a man after discovering and understanding what he had previously concealed from her. In our society, it's much more acceptable for a man to leave a woman. A married woman typically doesn't leave her man even if he's deceitful, squanders money that is not his own, tells lies, and is unfaithful.

Perhaps I should have been born in the next century, or be more like my Jewish school friends, who are independent and able to make decisions regarding their own lives. I am a young, educated Bedouin woman. I have two young sons, and I am raising them the way I believe they should be raised. Now I feel the power coming back to me, along with the decision to pursue a graduate degree in educational counseling. Suddenly, everything happened so fast: I enrolled in university, was invited for an admissions interview, and got accepted. At first, the instructors didn't understand why I sat in class next to the Bedouin girls. I look like the Jewish students, my Hebrew is excellent; the assignments I write at night in the cramped room where my sons sleep are good, and I know that when I get a bit more organized, they will be even better. I am a perfectionist, sometimes too much, but I believe that's how I can achieve every goal

I set for myself. Here I started several sentences with the word "I". Among Bedouins in general, and Bedouin women in particular, there is no such word. It's all "we" and "what will they say" and "it's not acceptable" and "in our family", and every other word is "honor". The problem is that they and I understand this word [honor] slightly differently. I respect the honor they speak of and refrain from talking to any man, even if he's an old friend or a family member. I don't mind refraining from stirring up trouble where it's not necessary, but I understand true honor differently, as the red-headed teacher used to tell us: respect for a person, for their freedom, for their right to choose what suits them.

I don't live in the clouds and I'm well aware of the challenges ahead of me. For example, I can imagine the expression on my father's face when I tell him that I want to leave his home with my two sons to a small, separate apartment of my own. I'll explain to him that it's impossible to pursue advanced degrees when we have to turn off the lights at eight in the evening in the shared room where I live with them, so that the little ones can sleep. It will be very difficult for him, but I believe that eventually he will understand and agree. I think again about my red-headed psychology teacher. She once told me that my curiosity along with my ability to give and empathize with others will eventually lead me to her profession. I don't think she knew exactly how tough this journey could be.

CHAPTER II
Growth from Loss and Bereavement

Introduction: Compartmentalized Grief

My journey into widowhood did not descend upon me suddenly. For a year and a half, we battled against a demonic force whose arms cruelly ensnared us. In April 2004, my three children and I were left with the bitter realization that we had lost the man we so dearly loved. A new reality, one we did not choose, became the daily backdrop to which I awoke each morning, clinging to remnants of a past that no longer held any tangible, living presence. The question of who I was without the man with whom I had shared my life was not hypothetical, but a painful task I was forced to confront. Everything changed; nothing was as it had been, nor was I the same person. The meaning of life, bereavement, orphanhood, and widowhood, along with endless longing — these were the building blocks with which I had to reconstruct my home and my identity anew. I appreciated the dedication and goodwill of the rehabilitation workers at the Ministry of Defense in accompanying bereaved families, but I knew that the task of discovering my path forward was mine alone, and no one could tackle that undertaking for me.

The journey of mourning and adaptation is fundamentally universal, yet uniquely personal to each family, and to each individual. Back then, I was not yet aware of the religious, cultural, and societal differences that colored this journey. Seven years passed, and my life settled into a different blessed routine — a family routine where children grow, marry, and bring new babies into the world. Their sweet scent cries for hugs and soothing, and their warm bodies slightly ease the pain and offer comfort.

A random story about a Bedouin widow of the IDF, left childless, who remarried as a second wife and needed fertility treatments which the state refused to provide, ignited in me a blaze of sorrow, compassion, and anger. The anger felt futile against the state's guidelines that fertility treatments are provided only to single women or first wives. "Let the widow go to court," they suggested when I sought to advocate for the woman and act on her behalf. This advice likely came from someone who had only encountered Bedouin women in the hallways of health clinics or the vast parking lots of shopping centers outside the city. Initially, I wanted to meet the widow, to hear her story. Gradually, I was drawn into meetings filled with pain and power with other Bedouin widows whose husbands had fallen in combat or passed away during military service. My life intersected with theirs in a shared personal pain, which had already become an inseparable part of me, while simultaneously exposing me to lives profoundly different from anything I had previously known.

The Ministry of Defense, quite rightly, refused to provide me with the names of Bedouin IDF widows. Had my name been shared, I would have contested the violation of my right to privacy. For two years, I roamed around the expanses of the Negev, armed with connections within the Bedouin community who believed in me and helped me reach these women to intimately understand their lives after loss. It took another two years until the academic papers I co-authored with my research partner, Dr. Yaarit Bokek-Cohen, on IDF widows were published.

Senior rehabilitation officials read in our work what field practitioners had long understood — i.e., not every change is revolutionary. Sometimes, it is a shift in awareness from which action emerges.

I promised the Bedouin IDF widows that when writing about them, I would conceal their identities as much as possible. They have compelling reasons to remain in the shadows and avoid exposure. They do not appear at official memorial ceremonies or public gatherings. Their lives are interwoven with daily acts of resilience: they wake up every morning to a reality filled with challenges, gathering strength to care for their children, their homes, and their new lives. They do this in the face of a restrictive environment, whose constraints they are no longer willing to accept without question.

Sometimes, you come to a halt, unable to take another step. What you have seen, heard, and felt anchors your feet to the ground. You find yourself stranded in an unfamiliar place, marveling at a world so close yet unseen until now. The stories of the Bedouin IDF widows not only stir emotions but also provoke difficult questions. How can an institution, with its structured protocols, deliver such devastating news with cultural sensitivity? How do these widows navigate a social landscape where their recognized grief is not acknowledged? Their stories differ from those of the Jewish widows I've known, yet their pain is so strikingly similar.

Faiza

At Your Home

One of the fellows from the Bedouin leadership group at the Mandel Center told me about Faiza. "She's a widow who has no fear," he remarked. I tried calling her several times, but received no response. As I later learned, Bedouin women typically do not answer calls from unknown numbers. Eventually, someone volunteered to go to her, and only after he confirmed my number displayed on her screen, did she answer the phone. Faiza's voice sounded hesitant. Life had taught her to be cautious, especially after Ali was killed. Yet, there was a hint of curiosity in her voice and a readiness to take a risk. I offered to meet at a location of her choosing. Suddenly, I heard her say, "At your house." The silence on the other end of the line and the hesitation were now mine. My private life felt separate from the scope of my research, although I was aware of the implied characteristics that linked us. Suddenly, the concept of reciprocity struck me: privacy in exchange for privacy. Buber's description of human reciprocal relations, even in asymmetrical situations,[12] helped me. "I'll come in my jeep," she said, "Your village is just past our junction, we are neighbors."

One week later, we sat in my kitchen. She recounts her experiences, and I listen intently, absorbing her story with a thirst, feeling her strength surge into me. I met a woman who had merely sought to manage her household quietly, in peace. However, life swept her up like a torrential desert flood, and she stood firm and withstood the deluge. I capture her story in my own words. My

---

[12] Buber, M. (1981). *The Hidden Dialogue: On Man and Being.* Jerusalem: Bialik Institute.

palette of words seems eager to further highlight her delicate, soft, and sensitive outlines — those that are vividly captured in spoken conversation but do not find adequate expression in the formal language of interviews. I know these are my words, yet I allow them to flow from me, then, wrap around and envelop her narrative. She speaks, and I walk with her story through the landscape of my childhood, feeling it in my bones. It resonates within me all the way until the narrow, black road separating her house from mine blurs and disappears.

Faiza's Story

Yellow Hills

Almost all year round, the hills where my family pitched their tents were cloaked in a dull, dusty yellow. Only after the occasional winter rain fell did their color shift to a bright, refreshing green. First, the tall Asphodelus appeared along with blooming Drimia aphylla spikes, followed by delicate carpets of flowers covering the yellowish, loess soil. The slopes of the hills were strewn with small stones that scratched our bare feet, and among them, almost hidden, was a bit of crumbled loose earth.

The first heat wave of the season, sometimes arrived before spring, drying out all the plants, leaving only the sturdy tamarisks, large broom shrubs, and the eucalyptus grove planted by the Jews who had come to the Negev. The trees had been there since the days when my grandfather wandered with his sheep, correspondingly to the seasons, roaming from the northern Negev to the Ramla area. My older brother said the eucalyptus trees were brought from Australia to drain the swamps. When I asked what a swamp was, he explained it was a place with lots of mud, like the big dam in the Wadi before

Rahat. Back then, I thought those trees — the eucalyptus with their sharp, red-green leaves — were as strange as the two Romanian women with yellow hair I saw when we went to the market in Rahat. Mother said one of them was the wife of a dentist who had studied in Romania, and the other was the third wife of Naif, the wealthy contractor, the one with the big trucks.

Behind the road alongside the grove, you could see the Muslim cemetery. My aunt used to tell us that after people were buried there, demons would roam around, seeking to harm and punish those who committed wrongdoings during their lives, especially those who didn't follow Allah's commandments. Closer to Kibbutz Shoval stood the old British police station, which no one would enter or leave because its doors were barricaded with heavy planks. I couldn't comprehend how a building could remain standing intact, yet uninhabited. From our tent, on the side where the sun rises, you can see the sprawling Bedouin city of Rahat; and in the opposite direction is Kibbutz Mishmar HaNegev, where the big tractors rumble down the nearby dirt road, stirring up clouds of dust that fly directly in my eyes, even when I quickly dash back into the tent.

I grew up with four sisters and six brothers. We were eleven children altogether. I was the youngest of the girls, with one brother younger than me by a year. Mother called him "Prince." I was his sister, but certainly no princess — just another kid: sometimes good, sometimes bad. Father often confused my name with that of my older sister. I suspect that hers was the only girl's name he remembered.

Once, my older sister told me we used to have another brother who was born very small. He died before he turned one because of a respiratory illness that sometimes affects babies born prematurely. I was afraid I might die too because I was very small, and Mother would often say I was too skinny. My sister reassured me, saying there's a vaccine-like injection nowadays, so people don't die from that illness anymore. Many years later, when my heart was shattered because of what happened to me, and I could hardly breathe, it was my sister who came to help so I would be a little less afraid.

I attended school until the sixth grade. I was a good student and could read and write Arabic beautifully. We only began learning Hebrew in the fifth grade, two hours a week. I understood a few words in Hebrew, but we didn't learn to read. When I finished elementary school, my parents told me, "Enough. You're done. Girls don't need more schooling." No one from the Ministry of Education visited us or explained that, by law, girls must also continue their education. So, I remained home with my three older sisters. We helped our mother with all her chores and played as well. My eldest sister was already married to my uncle. My three other sisters made sure to stay at home since their marriages were already being arranged. I could still accompany my mother to the big health clinic in Rahat, stroll through the market, and stop by the shop across from the municipality where an old Bedouin woman, covered in blue tattoos, sold special soaps and jars filled with plants and pills designed to chase away negative thoughts.

Groom by Method of Exchange

When I was seventeen, my father chose a groom for me through an exchange marriage (in Arabic, "Badal"). My father had a son and a daughter of marriageable age, and my uncle had a son and a daughter of similar ages. In exchange marriages, neither party needs to pay the other, and the wedding is less of an expense for both families. It's amusing because, in my uncle's family, there were three sets of twins, so the family always spoke in pairs. Ali was the older of the first pair of twin boys. His father already had many children from his two wives, so a "wedding by exchange" involving both a son and a daughter suited him perfectly.

Ali, who was two years older than me, had only studied up to the fourth grade. I opposed the marriage not just because of his lack of education, but primarily because of his family. His father was married to two women: the first was Ali's mother, and the second was my older sister. I told my father, "How can I call Ali's second mother 'Aunt' when she's my older sister?" I also had a negative view of polygamous marriages. I believed that if a man married two women, he would inevitably love one wife more than the other. I wanted to marry a husband who would have only one wife, and for my children to grow up without another woman and her children around.

Back then, I didn't really know Ali. My sister would visit us with her children, but I had only seen the first wife, Ali's mother, once or twice at a family event. At those gatherings, we girls didn't interact with the boys from the extended family, so I had no way of knowing if Ali was a good match for me. I was afraid that because he hadn't received a robust education, he wouldn't permit his own children study. Ali worked as a plasterer's assistant with his uncle. They told me he spoke politely and didn't cause trouble. In the end, I agreed to marry him. I had considered someone else in the family who had always wanted to marry me, but they lived near the city of Arad, an hour away from our family home, and I wanted to stay close to my parents. Less than a year after the agreements and the engagement, Ali and I got married.

After the wedding, I saw that I did love Ali. In our tradition, love isn't all that important; a couple must remain together after their marriage, no matter what. But we enjoyed each other's company, and being together with Ali was much nicer than I had expected. In the evenings, Ali would come home from work, and if there was still light, we would sit outside and try to read a newspaper in Arabic. I could read Arabic better than Ali could, and he would make me laugh every time he managed to read. I could tell that he appreciated my wisdom and knowledge. Our relationship was different from what I had seen between my mother and father. He would talk to me and tell me about his day, and I could see that he was intelligent, despite his having very little formal education. We soon had three children, and Ali would help me with shopping, as well as whatever else I asked of him. The problem was that he didn't bring home much money. Sometimes, plasterers from the village of Dura near Hebron would under bid in order to secure a particular job, so the Bedouin contractor Ali worked for paid him very little. We talked about how someone with a steady monthly salary could eventually buy a car and maybe even build a house.

I can't quite remember exactly when he first began talking about serving in the Army. I told him that enlisting in the Israeli Army was "Haram" (forbidden). Israeli soldiers fight against Palestinians near Hebron, Nablus, and Ramallah, so should anything bad happen to him, God wouldn't come to our aid. My father said that Bedouins should not join the Army and that enlisting in the IDF was a disgrace. But in Ali's family, they believed the Army belonged to our State, and that it's an honor to serve as a soldier. Especially since there was no Intifada at that time, and everything was quiet, I suggested my husband try to join the police force. I liked the police. They kept traffic orderly and helped when someone stole or caused trouble. Ali went to the police station in Rahat and spoke with the officer, but it turned out he did not have the required formal education to become a policeman. In the end, Ali told me he would become a tracker in the IDF's Bedouin Battalion. The next day he returned home already dressed in Army uniform. In our tradition, a wife does not oppose her husband's decisions.

Bitter Bread

Ali would come home from the Army every two weeks and stay for a week each time. At first, my family had opposed his enlistment, but they began to appreciate him when they saw how well we got along and were also making progress financially. Sometimes, Ali would bring groceries for my mother, finding them at a good price, and he never asked her for money in return. I could see Ali evolving and growing; he was reading better and even reading stories to our eldest child, who was already five, from the books and workbooks I had bought for him.

Ali said he wanted to advance and transfer to the Border Police. The trackers only patrolled along the border, but the Border Police fought with weapons. He was released from the tracker unit to join the Border Police, but they didn't accept him because he hadn't completed enough years of study. More importantly. he couldn't read or write in Hebrew.

Nevertheless, Ali didn't give up. He and other Bedouin soldiers went to a military camp in the Galilee that was like a school. Female soldiers who knew some Arabic taught them like schoolteachers. Ali described how they wore Army uniforms with gray cords hanging from the left shoulder strap of their uniform, and tried very hard to teach. Ali spoke of them with respect, even though they were women. He said they had quite a lot of patience and didn't mind working all day to help the soldiers succeed in their studies. Sometimes, it seemed like they were simply playing word games and asking riddles, but it was all so the soldiers would remember the words. I saw Ali becoming more educated and was happy for him.

After four months of study, Ali enlisted in the Border Police. He served in various places: Hebron, near Gaza, around Jerusalem, Bethlehem, and many other challenging locations. I knew he also helped Palestinians at checkpoints, especially women and children who needed to reach the hospital in Jerusalem. The problem was that we already had seven children, I was pregnant again, and it was difficult for me to wait for him for so many days. Ali requested a transfer closer to home so he could help me with the children and complete his high school studies. After many requests, he received approval to transfer to the Border Police base near Kiryat Gat. I felt like God had blessed my family.

All those years, I remained at home. Our women bring children into the world and care for them; that's their whole life. I was thirty years old, a Bedouin woman living in our shack in the unrecognized villages in the Negev near Rahat, just like all the other women around me. I didn't have a driver's license and hardly ever left our property. Ali brought everything home and took me to the hospital every time I needed to give birth.

My eighth daughter, Ilham, was born twelve years after our wedding. When it was time for me to give birth, Ali was in the Army, so his twin brother took me to the hospital. On the day the baby and I were discharged, Ali arrived in his uniform. The hospital guard didn't even check him at the gate like they usually do with all the other Bedouins. I had no idea that my life would soon change in an instant. I brought my new baby home, wrapped in a colorful blanket with drawings of little chicks that Ali had brought me for Noor's birth four years earlier. I was exhausted after giving birth and relieved that we held the celebration for the new baby only after forty days. Ali adjusted his Army schedule a bit and stayed home for an entire week after I came back from the hospital. He then returned home for a few more days before heading back to the Army so he could be back for the party.

On the morning of the celebration, I made up the bed where he slept so that if he came home after working all night, he could lie down and rest right away. I went to his mother's house to bake a bread called "al-Saadi." It's a large, thin bread into which rice and sheep fat are rolled. His mother lived very close to our house. In the afternoon, I had an appointment at the well-baby clinic and planned to invite his family over to celebrate with us afterward. Around noon, I asked my five-year-old son, Imad, to go home and see if his father had arrived. I asked him to tell his dad to come and say hello. I wanted to see him because my heart always felt lighter whenever he was with me. Ilham lay wrapped in her chick-patterned blanket, and I quietly worked all morning.

When the dough was nearly finished, and I had only five or six loaves left to bake, I heard a loud noise outside. I stepped out and saw many Army vehicles by our house, along with Ali's brother's cars. I tried calling Ali, but he didn't answer. Suddenly, Nasser, Ali's twin brother, came over, and I saw he was crying. Nasser was a friend to me, not just a brother-in-law. He always helped me when Ali was away. I asked him, "Why are you crying?" Nasser looked at me with the saddest eyes I had ever seen and told me that his brother had died in a car accident.

A curtain of darkness fell over my face. I remember the warm body of little Ilham, whom I took out of the crib to bring home. She was crying. At that moment, I couldn't wait to nurse her. Even though it was midday, I ran back home as if I were alone in a dark cave.

Dark Despair

When I arrived home, the entire field next to the house was filled with cars. Some people went to Ali's father's place, while others came to me. I don't remember who arrived or what they said. At that time, I didn't speak Hebrew, and the female soldiers who arrived didn't know Arabic. I didn't see him when he died. I think if they'd asked if I wanted to see his body, I would have refused. Women do not attend funerals. About two hundred women came to see me, and we stayed together for three days in a tent and then in the house. My eldest daughter was ten, and Omar, my eldest son, after whom my husband was known as "Abu Omar" (father of Omar) and I as "Umm Omar" (mother of Omar), was nine years old. I remember it like it was yesterday — he played and laughed. I told myself he didn't understand. I wept in my heart, fearing that perhaps Omar was unaware of what had happened. I cried for my children more than for myself. Little Ilham was passed from one set of hands to another. The women brought food to the house, and I looked at the yellow hills I loved, but all I could see was darkness, both in my eyes and in my heart. Eventually, everyone left. My father asked me what I wanted to do, but I didn't know what the future would look like. I waited for Ali to come back, even though I knew it wouldn't happen. After three days, the older children returned to school. I cooked, did laundry, and took care of the children, thinking those were the only things I knew how to do. My older sister, who was also like a second mother to Ali, came to visit me every day, as did my mother-in-law and sisters-in-law. But at night, I was left all alone.

On the Army's website they wrote in Hebrew: "Ali was a serious man, fulfilled all his duties, and made the right decisions whenever required. He had a talent for managing people and always looked after his subordinates in the best possible way. Ali was beloved in his unit. He had a big heart and many friends. Ali received a Certificate of Appreciation for his determination and high level of professionalism. Ali was killed at the end of a night shift in a car accident on his way back to the base to hand over the jeep and operational equipment to the next shift. Many accompanied him on his final journey — family members, community elders, soldiers and commanders, his fellow unit members. He leaves behind a wife, children, parents, and eight brothers and sisters." At the time, I didn't know that the Army had written about him, as I could not read Hebrew at all.

A Step Forward

A year later, I began learning to drive. In our community, women aren't supposed to drive, but I found it difficult to always rely on my brothers or Ali's brothers to take me and the children to the clinic or the market. The social worker from the Defense Ministry told me that Jewish widows have cars, and I'd feel better if I could occasionally leave our shack. I left my baby with my older sister, at her home, where she lived with Ali's mother, and headed to Be'er Sheva.

I have three brothers who helped me. They took me from my home in the Bedouin unrecognized villages near Mishmar HaNegev to Rahat, where I caught a transit van to Be'er Sheva. I had money I received monthly from the Army; however, I didn't tell my father anything about it. Now, my father was responsible for guarding my honor and ensuring I didn't leave the house. Ali's father knew I was learning to drive, so he went to my father and told him I was taking lessons. My father was furious and sent my brother to tell me I could not continue. I went to Rahat to see my father and told him that if my husband were alive, I wouldn't need to drive. But now I needed a license, because who else would pick up the children after a school trip? Or if my son fell ill, who would take us to the doctor? My father replied, "If your husband were alive, that would be fine. But now you're a widow, and I'm responsible for you. I won't allow you to drive because it's forbidden." I replied, "Alright, Father, I won't learn to drive," but I continued with my lessons, nevertheless. A man who knew me saw me driving, but he must have thought I was someone else because he didn't say a word. Maybe he was afraid that if he spoke up and it wasn't me, people would accuse him of lying. I passed the driving test on my fourth attempt without anyone finding out. My license arrived in the mail at my parents' address. Luckily, my brother opened the mail and didn't tell my father anything.

I bought a car after finishing the mandatory period of supervised driving together with a companion. I didn't have anyone to accompany me anyway, so I simply waited for the time to pass. I was unaware of my rights through the Ministry of Defense, so I bought the car solely using my own money. I remember buying it three days before the "Twin Towers disaster" in America. I had been at home, thrilled, but also scared. What frightened me most was my father's reaction. I sat at home, glued to the TV, watching the world unravel through the repeated images of planes crashing into the towers and the buildings collapsing. My heart ached for the people who died, and I couldn't help but think that maybe some of them had small children like mine, who were now left without their father.

Suddenly, my brother showed up. He said his car had broken down and asked to borrow mine. I handed him the keys without saying a word, not even mentioning the cost of gas. Two days later, my father arrived from Rahat to our small village. He walked on foot, perhaps to check on his properties. He noticed a car he didn't recognize parked by my house and approached a laborer from Hebron who worked for my brother to inquire about who owned the car. The laborer replied, "The car belongs to Faiza, the widow." My father didn't speak. He was furious but did not enter my house. Instead, he told my brother that he wanted to see me. I was terrified and couldn't sleep the entire night. In the morning, I sent the children to school and took the two little ones with me to see my father in Rahat. My father asked me why I had bought a car. I didn't answer him because it would not matter what I responded. My father continued to look at me, and when enough time had passed without a response, he said, "Now you have a license and a car. You mustn't give the keys to your brothers. They'll waste your gas and won't pay you back. They'll also park illegally in Be'er Sheva, and then you'll end up with fines from the police that you'll have to pay. The car is only for you and your children." My father is a religious man. He says you mustn't take from orphans. He is kind-hearted and compassionate toward widows and orphans and wants to protect me.

I started driving and suddenly felt like I had wings. The first thing I did was drive to Neighborhood Seven in Rahat, to a place called Majd Al-Kamlat — "A Step Forward." There was a kind woman there named Roni who taught Arabic and Hebrew classes. I didn't tell anyone in my family where I was going; I simply got into the car with my two little ones and drove off. I no longer cared what the women in my neighborhood would say. Everyone already knew I drive a car and that my father approved. Nurah, who works at the health clinic where I take my children for check-ups and vaccines, encouraged me and told me that her husband had promised her a 500-shekel gift if she got her driver's license. I know her parents are from Ramla, which is a little different from our community, but I was glad to hear her kind words. I felt like "A Step Forward" was not just the name of my class but the direction my entire life was heading.

Ministry of Defense

After the tragedy, I was told that the Ministry of Defense would assist me. Someone came and helped me fill out forms, and soon enough, the money did arrive in the bank. Before my husband died, I had never set foot in the bank. He handled everything because we had a joint account. I knew how to withdraw money from the machine because he had shown me once, teaching me as if it was a game. I knew what to do, but I couldn't understand the Hebrew text. Every month, I received letters in the mail about my rights, but everything was written in Hebrew. Nothing was in Arabic. I like the Ministry of Defense representative; she is very kind. But before I knew Hebrew, I couldn't communicate with her at all. Once, my friend Norah from the clinic went online to the Ministry of Defense webpage. She thought the benefits would be listed there in Arabic, but all she found was a single sentence written in large Hebrew print: "A seeing eye, a listening ear, and an understanding heart." Norah translated the phrase for me. It was beautiful. We understood this message was written for the Jewish widows because if it were meant for us too, it would certainly have been written in Arabic as well. I realized that I had to learn Hebrew because my rights were all written in Hebrew, and if I didn't learn it, I would risk losing them. Ultimately, I went to the nearby Steimatzky book store, bought a Hebrew-Arabic dictionary, and for several days, and spent several days meticulously translating the benefits page, word by word. I spent perhaps an hour looking at every single word, writing the translation in the margins.

I paid for the Hebrew lessons with Roni with my own money, and I also covered the driving licensing fees from my bank account. Once, during a trip with other widows, I met Fadel, a Druze gentleman from the North. He gave us his phone number and told us to call if we needed anything. When my eldest daughter got married, I called him, and he told me that the Ministry of Defense provides financial assistance for the wedding of an IDF orphan. Many women don't know their rights. Before I learned Hebrew, I missed out on many of mine. Today, I can read slowly, little by little. Once, we were given gift vouchers for a book at Steimatzky. My eldest was ten years old. I wanted to read her stories in Arabic. I went to Steimatzky and asked if they had any books in Arabic. They said they didn't, but the saleswoman offered to special order them. That's how, for the first time, the store began to stock children's books in Arabic.

My story is nearly at its end. I want to share one additional sad story that weighs heavily on my heart, as well as something else — something joyful.

Memorial Day and Day of Destruction

My husband, Ali, served in the Border Police. He had good friends there, and everyone loved him. We live in an unrecognized village, but everyone knows its name and where our house is located. Next to my house, I built a home for my son, who would soon be getting married.

On Memorial Day, they came from the Army and brought the Israeli flag, a small wreath, and a gift in a cardboard box — a book of poems in Hebrew with pictures of vivid red anemones and other flowers. They told me they'd never forget us or what Ali had given to the country. That was on Tuesday. On Thursday morning, fifty people arrived with tractors to demolish the house I'd built for my son. They were members of the Border Police. The soldiers who carried out the house demolition were from the Border Police, perhaps even the same soldiers who had served alongside my husband. They took action against an Army widow and orphans. Well, they truly didn't forget us, just as they had said…

Our Children

Seldom do all the children come home together at the same time. My yellow hills are just a place to them. In my head, I always count them and think about them. Suha, my eldest, was an excellent student and graduated with a full matriculation certificate. She got married and didn't continue her studies. Today, she has three children and works as a cashier. Next year, she'll start studying education at college. Omar graduated from high school with a matriculation diploma. He wanted to get married, but after his house was demolished, he now needs to wait. Omar doesn't want to study further and works as a welder. Yasmin is studying medicine in Romania, in her fourth year. In her first year, she studied in Jordan. They didn't treat her well because she was from Israel, so she decided to move to Romania and start over. Raud is in his fourth year of studying dentistry in Romania. He and Yasmin are in the same place in Romania, and he looks after her. Imad graduated with a matriculation diploma and is now serving in the IDF Givati Brigade. I think he'll become an officer. When I look at him, he reminds me of Ali, but he's just as smart and knowledgeable as his Jewish friends. Salem is studying to become an engineer. He's finished his first year at the technical college. Hakmeh finished twelfth grade and can become a nurse, or a teacher, or choose any other profession she wants. My little Ilham is going into eleventh grade. I still have the baby chick blanket I wrapped her in when I took her home from the hospital. I will never remarry or become anyone's second wife. I made that decision even before I married Ali.

Sana

Vibrant Greenery

"You must meet Sana," Amir, a Bedouin officer who had recently been discharged from the IDF and was working to encourage Bedouin youth to enlist, told me. His eyes lit up when he spoke about Sana. In his voice, I could hear not only affection for her but also deep respect. He described her as "very dynamic." At that point, I couldn't yet imagine how independent, self-assured, articulate, and clear she would be, describing the world around her with the same soft glow of crisp air after the rain. Amir gave me a well-rehearsed speech about his official role and left. I'm not sure if our meeting ended because of the phone call that interrupted our conversation or if the call gave him an excuse to leave without apologizing. On the sheets of paper where I had planned to write down my interview with him about Bedouin society's attitude toward young people enlisting in the Army, only Sana's phone number remained. What lingered in my memory was the image of his smiling eyes when he suggested I meet Sana, the widow of Ibrahim.

To my surprise, Sana immediately agreed to my request for a meeting. Even over the phone, I could sense her passionate temperament, which radiated strongly through her voice. Her Hebrew was fluent and robust. She was willing to come anywhere, almost anytime. I invited Sana to meet me at my workplace in the afternoon, where programs for the development of local leadership are held, including in Bedouin communities. The location is one floor above the offices of the Ministry of Defense's Rehabilitation and Commemoration Department, which oversees care for bereaved families. Her presence wouldn't seem out of place, and I hoped she would feel comfortable during our meeting. The woman I welcomed at the center's doors was dressed in traditional clothing, with her beauty shining through, though she took no special effort to emphasize it. When Sana began to talk about her childhood in the Judean Hills, I could imagine the fresh, vibrant greenery that surrounded her back then, a glow that remained with her even after life led her to the arid landscapes of the Negev.

Sana's Story

Within the Realms of Childhood

Most people only know the beautiful area where I was born through a car window. When I was watching over the sheep in the field, the cars looked like little boxes gliding down the mountain along the black road. My father's pickup truck constantly drove through the area. It's possible he didn't even have a license or auto insurance. My father saw and knew everything happening in the fields. The people in their cars couldn't see the sheep giving birth or Na'uja, the clever one, leading the flock with the big bell hanging around her neck. We used to wander with the sheep between Gadera to Ramla.

Our tent was always in the same place near K'far Bilu, close to the houses of the Jews. When I was little, there was no separation between their land and ours. Our neighbors spoke a slightly strange, funny kind of Arabic. Mother said they came from

Morocco, where the people spoke a language with several words similar to ours. We understood them, and they understood us. In the winter, when the heavy rain fell it didn't stop for an entire week. Their mother brought us two old blankets. The day before their son celebrated his thirteen-year-old ceremony, which they called a "Bar Mitzvah," my mother helped them prepare the food, even though she was Bedouin.

There were five children in our nuclear family: my older brother Musa and I, followed by two more boys and a girl. My father had no extended family in Israel because all his uncles moved to Jordan during the "Nakba."[13] We belong to the al-Azazmeh tribe, scattered throughout the unrecognized villages near Yeruham. When I was seven, my parents decided to leave the good place we lived and return to the Negev because my father wanted us to study in a Bedouin school. We moved there, and I no longer went out with the sheep. Musa was already eight and a half and had not yet started school. My father said that nowadays, everyone needs to know how to read and write. My mother wasn't educated and had never attended school. She knew how to cook, and care for us. She even knew a few words in Hebrew that the Jewish neighbors taught her. Only my father was allowed to handle all the arrangements and shopping outside the house.

When I began first grade, I was a year older than all the other children. I didn't look any older and like all the other students, my brother and I wore blue, gray, and pink tracksuits from the Thursday market in Be'er Sheva. I wasn't afraid of the teachers or the principal. I succeeded in learning quickly and never gave the teachers a reason to punish me. I missed the fields near K'far Bilu and my

---

[13] Nakba, "the Catastrophe", refers to the Palestinian term for the departure of approximately 700,000 Palestinians from the land during Israel's War of Independence, which turned them into refugees.

quiet time with the sheep, but I also loved studying and was proud of the excellent report cards I brought home to my father.

In my family, there were seven people, but Mother also cooked for the old man who lived alone on the other side of the hill and joined us to eat every day. Mother would greet him, invite him to sit with the men, and send me or my younger sister over with a large plate of food. Once, I asked her why she gave him food every day, and she said that Allah blesses the generous.

My world turned upside down and changed when I was ten, towards the end of third grade. The days grew longer, and even after coming back from school, we had plenty of daylight hours left to play outside before we all went back home. On Friday, my father sent us some boxes of food with a neighbor who lived nearby, so that Mother could start cooking before dark. The neighbor told us that my father would return a little later because they had received one more urgent job. Mother called me over, and I helped her sort the groceries and put everything away in its place. There was a sack of rice, a sack of potatoes, and boxes of vegetables.

At seven-thirty in the evening, when it was already dark outside, I saw the lights of many pickup trucks racing towards our shack. I didn't recognize most of the friends who got out of the vehicles. They were shouting and talking loudly about an accident near Be'er Sheva. A truck had crashed into my father's car. I ran to find my mother and saw her lying down as if she was dead.

My father's life ended when he was thirty-five. My mother became a widow at thirty-one. I never imagined that I would become a widow at that same age.

Coping

We were left alone in the shack my father had built for us, near a few other families from the al-Azazmeh tribe. Although we're from this tribe, we didn't have any close family in the area. In our culture, a widow isn't allowed to live alone without family, so we moved to live near my uncle in the Segev Shalom area. Early in the morning, while it was still dark outside, a contractor's pickup truck would arrive to transport the women to work in the fields. My mother would travel with them, and I would wake my brothers and take them to my aunt so I could make it to school on time. On Fridays and Saturdays, the three older children and Mother would travel to work in the fields near the Dead Sea. It was so hot that I felt like my body was burning up. The money Mother earned was not enough for us, so when I started high school, I worked nights in a carrot packing plant and went to school in the morning.

At that time, there was no high school near our village, and I was offered the chance to attend a high school further away. I was the only girl on the bus and would sit alone in the back to stay away from the boys. That's how I traveled to school from ninth to twelfth grade — thirty boys and me. Mother encouraged me to study even though she couldn't read or write herself. Every day, she would ask if we had any homework. My brother Musa struggled with his studies, so I helped him and did his homework for him, even though he was in a higher grade.

Shortly before the summer break between eleventh and twelfth grade, my mother suggested I get a driver's license. I almost fainted when I heard her suggestion because, sometimes, we didn't even have money for food. I had no idea how she managed to save up the money for driving lessons. Only the boys from the wealthier families in my class were learning to drive. Perhaps Mother decided I should get a license because Musa wasn't a good student, and I could handle myself anywhere. Even at school, I succeeded in my studies despite barely sleeping at night. During the summer vacation, I learned to drive, always thinking about the money

Mother had saved for the lessons. Mother was right. I passed the test the first time and got my license. We didn't have a car, and there was no one to accompany me, but I had my license, and Mother said that one day we'd have a car too.

That summer, I was so focused on my driving lessons that I wasn't aware of a new problem. Since I started school a year later than the other kids, the Ministry of Education didn't approve my twelfth-grade studies because they only pay up to the age of eighteen. I think the principal told the head of the regional council about me because he called me into his office and gave me five thousand shekels so I could continue my education and finish high school. He said it was a scholarship for me. He looked at me as he handed me the envelope and asked me to come back and teach at the village school once I became a teacher. He said that would be a triumph for him.

After finishing high school, I enrolled at Kaye College in Be'er Sheva. In my heart, I hoped I wouldn't be accepted. I felt like I had no more energy to study, and the travel was difficult for me. I knew that several families had started asking my uncle if I was willing to marry their son. Mother would not concede and said I had to continue studying. I took the psychometric test and was accepted. I spent three successful years studying there. My Hebrew improved significantly. I had almost no free time because I paid part of my tuition through a scholarship from Perach, which is given to students who assist struggling children. The student I tutored lived in the town of Kuseifa, about ten kilometers from our home, and I always had to find a way to get there. I was lucky that Ibrahim, my brother's friend, lived with his family not far from there. Many times, he offered to drive me to Kuseifa Sometimes he waited to take me back, especially when it started to get dark. I imagined that's how Father would have driven and helped me if he hadn't died in an accident when I was a little girl.

"I've Already Loved You for Five Years"

At our school, the boys who graduated with a high grade-point average went straight to university. The best students from the Construction and transportation contractors' families went to Hungary, Romania, Germany, and Russia to study medicine, while others studied in Jordan. The girls studied at universities in Bethlehem and Hebron or at Kaye College and Achva College. The weaker students went to work or joined the Army. When my older brother Musa finished his high school studies, he enlisted in the Army. Mother didn't want him to join because she was afraid for him. At the beginning of his military service, Musa's salary was low, but he was satisfied. He had many friends, and the commanders said Musa was a good and disciplined soldier. After completing officer training, he had enough money to support Mother and get married. Almost all his friends from the Army were married. I knew that Ibrahim, his friend who also served in the Army, had already married twice, and divorced his second wife.

One day, the phone in our house rang. I was sitting in the living room, writing a paper for one of my college professors. I picked up the phone and heard Ibrahim's voice on the other end. I told him that Musa wasn't back from the Army yet. He laughed and said he wanted to talk to me, not Musa. I didn't understand what he wanted to discuss with me. My heart pounded because in our culture it's not customary for a man to speak directly to a woman. Ibrahim told me that someone wanted to marry me. My first question was whether the man was married. Ibrahim answered honestly that the man who wanted me was already married. I was furious with him and felt insulted. "Why would I marry a married man?" I asked him. I told him I was educated, studying in college, and that there were men who wanted me. At first, I didn't care who had sent him to call me. After I calmed down a bit, I asked who the man was. Ibrahim refused to tell me. Finally, he gave in and said it was Ahmed, his sister's husband. My blood rushed to my face, and I felt it burn with shame. I asked him not to call me again because there was no chance that I would marry a married man as his second wife. I wanted to hang up the phone. I was disappointed that he was willing to speak on behalf of his brother-in-law so that I would become a second wife.

I don't understand how I didn't hang up, because there was silence on the other end of the line. Suddenly, Ibrahim said, "It's me." Another moment of silence followed. I could see him clearly in my mind — a strong, kind, and generous man. Mother trusted him, and once she even told me he reminded her of my father. I remembered my father's gentle face but never thought they looked alike. Ibrahim waited, and I stayed silent. Then I heard him say, "I've loved you for five years. Now that I've revealed the secret that's been in my heart, I won't ever give up on you, even if you run as far away as you can." I asked Ibrahim for a week to think about his offer. Ibrahim said two days should be enough. After two days, I agreed.

Mother surprised me again. Despite her fondness for Ibrahim, she said it wouldn't be wise to marry him. "You deserve to be someone's first wife. You're beautiful, educated, and young." My brother Musa didn't want to interfere and said I should do what I wanted. Our relatives insisted it wasn't a good idea to marry him because the girls from our tribe usually married within our own, and he was from a different family. Ibrahim called every day. He said he wanted me and that he was willing to kill anyone who opposed it. I don't think he meant it literally, but he also understood that the family had to agree. After two weeks, all the men in the family went to Musa's house, and Ibrahim brought the most important sheikh to talk to them about me. They sat in the guest room for several hours. I waited in Musa's bedroom with his wife and their baby, feeling very tense. In my heart, I already wanted Ibrahim, but I knew I didn't have the final say. When they finally emerged from the Shig, it was agreed that we would marry.

I was proud of Ibrahim and felt his unwavering determination to achieve what he wanted in life. Within a month, we were engaged, and a month later, by the end of October, when I returned for my final year of college, I was already married.

"Like Sisters"

I moved into the large house that Ibrahim built with the money he earned in the Army. His first wife lived on the first floor and already had six children, while I lived on the second floor. In truth, Ibrahim had married a second wife before me, and they had two daughters together, but he divorced her about a year before we got married. So, I entered his home as his second wife, not his third.

In the first year, Ibrahim would spend one night with me and the next with his first wife. We, the two wives, were like sisters, like friends. When I entered the house, I would linger on her floor before heading upstairs to mine. I did my practical training at an elementary school not far from home, and the principal asked me to teach ten hours as well. I would come back tired in the afternoon, and she would invite me to eat with her so that I could rest immediately afterward. I was pregnant, and soon after, our first child, Kaid was born. She was a quiet and kind woman, and I felt she genuinely cared for me.

A year after the wedding, she gave me Ibrahim's clothes and said she no longer wanted him to sleep with her and that it would be better if he only slept with me. Ibrahim didn't agree to this arrangement. A man needs to divide his nights equally so that all his wives are happy and there are no problems in the household. In the end, we came to an arrangement where he would visit her and lie with her, and then come to me. We were both content with this arrangement, and when I was pregnant with my second child, she was pregnant with her seventh. It worked well for both of us. I know some women fight and curse, but in our home, we got along well. Ibrahim took me and the older children on a vacation to Turkey, while the younger children stayed home with his first wife, who never left the house. We traveled a lot within Israel too.

Ibrahim had many ideas about how to move forward and earn more money. He spoke with Jewish friends he knew and Bedouins from the North who had served with him. After completing his high school education in Tel Aviv at an Army school, he knew how to handle finances and wasn't afraid of anything. He suggested we start two businesses: a restaurant in Kuseife and a butcher shop. I had the energy and strength to help him, even though I continued teaching at the school. Ibrahim extended his Army leaves, and we opened a shop. People would come to buy from us because of the good prices and because Ibrahim was so kind to them — helping them carry their purchases and taking an interest in each one. I felt like the sun was shining on my life.

Ibrahim bought me a mobile phone, and on the nights that he was in the Army, we would talk for hours. I would tell him about school and the children, and he would tell me about his friends in the Army. We planned to travel to Jordan, but he didn't get permission from the Army. We thought that perhaps when he was discharged, we could visit Petra and Amman and also see my father's uncles. I dreamed of us traveling to the holy city of Mecca together as well.

During Ramadan, at Eid al-Fitr, Ibrahim got some time off. We were with all the children at his parent's house when suddenly his friend called, asking if he could cover for him until Sunday. "I'll be home on Sunday," he promised me. He packed up to return to the Army and asked me to head back home as well, explaining that he didn't want me to travel alone with all the children. By then, I was already an experienced and skilled driver, and even when the kids fought in the car, I managed them well. In the end, we returned that night, and Ibrahim left for the Army. The next evening, he called me at eight o'clock. He was already out on patrol and said he'd call again when they got back. I fell asleep waiting for his phone call.

Black Morning

I woke up in the morning because someone was standing in my room, calling my name. I saw Pini, the commander of the Bedouin Trackers Unit, and my brother Musa. They were standing by my head, crying. "What happened?" I asked. I thought maybe Ibrahim's father or mother had died. They told me, "No, it's Ibrahim. He's dead. He was on patrol on the Arava Highway. They saw a suspicious vehicle on the other side of the road and stopped. Ibrahim got out to investigate, and then a car hit him." Ibrahim was wearing a dark military coat. It was winter and dark. He crossed the road and didn't see the car speeding up behind him. His friend shouted for him not to cross the road, but he didn't hear. The car hit him hard, causing internal bleeding. They brought a helicopter and flew him to Soroka Hospital in Be'er Sheva, but the doctors couldn't save his life. All this happened at night while I slept, waiting for his call. I started running down the stairs. Outside, there were many people from the Army. They stood by our house, and there was this kind of silence, like in a photograph or on TV when it stops working, and only the last image remains. I went into shock and climbed back upstairs to my floor. I remember nothing more.

The funeral was that day. He had promised to come home on Sunday, but I never imagined he would return dead. Women don't attend funerals, but I wanted to be close to him. When everyone left for the funeral, I ran outside. Someone agreed to my request and let me into his car. He said he would drive me on the condition that I wouldn't get out or cry. I promised him. It was incredibly difficult. I felt like I wanted to pull Ibrahim out of the grave. In our tradition, after a person dies, they are washed and wrapped in a white cloth, and no one is allowed to touch them. Then they are laid in the grave on a flat surface, and sand is sprinkled over them so that their body isn't harmed by the earth poured over them. Among the Jews, people visit the grave many times. In our culture, once the burial is complete, we leave and go away. It is forbidden to disturb the dead.

In the Army's records, it is written: "Ibrahim, aged thirty-eight at the time of his death, was the third son to his grieving parents. He was laid to rest in the Segev Shalom cemetery. He leaves behind three wives and thirteen children, both sons and daughters." But what they wrote down was not entirely accurate. He only had two wives, but he had orphaned children from three. The eldest wife, in her eighth month of pregnancy when tragedy struck, lost her baby due to the weight of the grief. He had twelve children because the child lost prematurely is not counted in the tally.

I returned home. We had three children when Ibrahim died: the youngest, just a year and a half, and the eldest, only five. Suddenly, the thought struck me that Ibrahim had bought many sheep for the holiday, which were now waiting in our butcher shop. Such work demanded a strong man. A woman alone wouldn't have the strength to lift the sheep and prepare their meat for sale. Amid the shock and confusion, I knew I needed to find a solution. That day, I knew that my life had completely changed.

When I arrived home, Noga from the Ministry of Defense was already there, waiting for me. She would be by my side for many years to come. Although she didn't speak Arabic, I knew enough Hebrew to share with her all the heavy burdens weighing on my heart.

There's No Such Thing as a "Half-Widow"

Ibrahim truly loved me and always took care of me. Before he died, he made sure to buy a plot of land for me because his first wife already had a home. He once joked, "You won't get anything if I die, because as far as the Army is concerned, you're not recognized." But Ibrahim made sure I was protected — He got life insurance for me and insurance for each child. I don't know many Bedouin men who take out insurance for anything other than their cars. A few days after his death, I was told that he had divided all his money equally between me and his first wife. It was important to him to put this in writing because he thought I wouldn't receive anything in court. Despite being recognized by the Army as his second wife, they still split the compensation between both of us, and each received only half. When I wanted to buy a car, they told me I was only entitled to half the money. I told the people at the Ministry of Defense that I wasn't a half-widow and that my children weren't half-orphans.

I went to the best lawyer in Be'er Sheva. A Jewish man with a large office in a tall building near the courthouse. This lawyer wins every case, especially against hospitals where doctors have been negligent. He sued the Ministry of Defense on my behalf and won. I believe I helped other Bedouin widows who are second or third wives because it takes tremendous courage to challenge the Ministry of Defense in court. When it came to Ibrahim's children, I decided how the money would be divided. Among us Bedouins, daughters receive only one-sixth of what the sons do. Nevertheless, I divided everything equally, as they would in a Jewish court, and not according to the Arab custom. Suddenly, at that moment, I remembered Na'uja, the sheep that always leads the flock. She's the smartest one, and although the others are less clever, they follow her along the right path.

To Remarry and Remain Alone

After Ibrahim was killed, my parents asked if I wanted to move back in with them. But I refused. I told them I wanted to stay in my own home, close to Ibrahim's family and his first wife, who was like a sister to me. Bader, Ibrahim's brother who was already married, approached me, and said he wanted us to marry. He promised, "I'll be like him, I'll love you just the same." I pondered Bader's proposal for about a year, and in the end, I agreed to marry him. He promised to help me build the house and be like a father to my children. Despite his promises, deep down, I knew I was making a grave mistake.

From the first day, I knew it wasn't right. Bader could never give me what his brother had. At first, he wanted me to sign documents at the bank to transfer the monthly payments I received from the Ministry of Defense to him. Noga told me that the money paid by the Ministry belongs to the widow and orphans and not to anyone else. Bader was furious. Once, when Noga visited, he came to talk to her along with another brother to confront her. But Noga stood her ground, unfazed by their words and unafraid of Bader. She calmly explained to them that this was the law of the land and that there wasn't a separate law for the Bedouins. Since that day, I haven't let him near my money.

Perhaps God loves me, and there's a purpose behind everything that happened. I had no time to rest, but I'm financially independent now. In the group of widows that meets at the Ministry of Defense, I'm the strongest participant and I help others to secure their rights. Sometimes, Noga asks me to speak with a widow who doesn't understand Hebrew, and explain everything to her. I feel that some of the strength I had when Ibrahim was alive has come back to me, but the joy has not returned.

I built a beautiful stone house on the plot of land Ibrahim bought for me, all by myself. I did everything on my own. Bader, my new husband, didn't lift a finger, or give me a single shekel. The house and the construction didn't interest him. If a man permits me to supervise male laborers working on the house — then he's not the right man to be my husband. A Bedouin woman shouldn't speak to the people building her home or be involved in business at all. But I did it. Despite the embarrassment, I had no choice. In the end, I was proud of myself.

My relationship with Bader was far from good. He only slept with his first wife and didn't arrange his nights like Ibrahim had. The children didn't like him. When he sat at home, he had no role. When my children caused trouble and I asked him to help, he did nothing. The children weren't afraid of him, needed nothing from him, and couldn't understand what he was even doing in our home. The people around us knew we weren't getting along. Every few months, I'd tell him to leave and that I wanted a divorce, and he begged me to stay. My friends at school told me that bearing his child would tether him more closely to my family. I became pregnant and went through it all alone. It wasn't like with Ibrahim, who touched my belly and wanted to feel the baby kicking.

One night, I felt the unmistakable need to give birth. Bader, who worked as a night guard, told me to wait until morning, because only then could he come to take me to the hospital. But by four in the morning, my contractions had grown fierce. I called him but couldn't wait any longer. I drove myself to the hospital, fighting through the contractions, and by nine o'clock, my baby was born. Bader finished his shift, and instead of coming to the hospital, he went home to eat. It wasn't until around noon that he finally showed up. When Bader walked in, I was lying weakly in bed after giving birth, and they had just taken the baby for check-ups. He asked, "When are you giving birth?" utterly unaware that I had already delivered our daughter hours earlier. Suddenly, I felt sharp pressure and began to bleed heavily. My life was in danger, and they rushed me to the operating room for an excruciating seven-hour surgery. The doctors could not find the source of the bleeding. I felt like my life was ending, and that my husband had never truly cared about his little girl who was just born. I don't even know where Bader was during those hours. I suspect he went back home to sleep.

Bader insists the child isn't his, so he refuses to pay a single shekel for her care. But I couldn't care less; I don't need him at all. This past June, during Ramadan, I made up my mind — I no longer wanted him in the house. He kept coming back every few days, begging me to return to him. Even the day before yesterday, he showed up again, but I've stopped speaking to him. I want to raise my children on my own. My older children with Ibrahim are already in high school, and the youngest is six and a half. I pursued a master's degree at a college in Tel Aviv but chose to stay on as a special education teacher because of the extra salary given to those working with the most challenging children.

Two of my brothers live in Switzerland. I traveled to Zurich with my four children. My brother Musa, with his six children, and my mother all came along too. Together, as a family — a party of twenty-seven — we went to a kosher restaurant because, like the Jews, we don't eat pork. I feel that my entire family respects me, and today, I no longer need to marry anyone. In my dreams, I travel with Ibrahim to the sacred city of Mecca or wander with him through Jordan. But in reality, I looked out the window of the warm, heated restaurant at the towering mountains, their snowy peaks glistening in the sun. The voices of the children around me are reminiscent of the bleating of the sheep we used to gather in the evenings before heading home.

CHAPTER III
Social Leadership in the Inner Courtyard

Introduction: Outside the Public Sphere

Since the earliest of times, the daily lives of desert women took place in the inner courtyard, secluded from the outside world. The aromatic array of meticulously arranged vegetables, petite cucumbers, and fragrant rice simmering in large pots standing over the crackling flames, amidst lamb meat roasting on the embers still covered with traces of loose earth, is where the whispered world of women was found. In the inner courtyard, shielded from the prying gaze of outsiders forbidden to tread near the tents, the shack, or the home dwelling without the escort of their male hosts, mothers instructed their daughters what Bedouin women were required to know. There, among piles of laundry, the girls giggled at the news brought by a messenger from a family seeking to betroth their son to one of the young women who was grown. At the heart of the inner courtyard, the mother-in-law, mother of the husband, formidably reigned, at times simultaneously juggling between caring for her young children and grandchildren. Before the advent of telephones, this was the hub of up-to-date information about everything happening in the neighborhood. Here, whispers carried news about the new doctor who arrived at the clinic, about the young man cruising in a luxury car after successfully delivering several shipments of "good stuff" (meaning, drugs) across the Wadi connecting Sinai to Jordan, or about another new bridal salon opening in the bustling city, or about "that guy" – may his name and his father's be erased – who went to Jordan "for business" and indulged in scandalous escapades with prostitutes or other women. For women, the perimeter of the tin fence surrounding the inner courtyard is also the perimeter of life. Beyond that, everything in the public realm, was intended for men alone.

How does female leadership, centered on public social reform without entering the male domain, blossom? Can societal change emerge from within the inner courtyard? The stories of Hanan and Hiba challenge this familiar notion precisely because they are religious, traditional women, who meticulously adhere to all commandments and prohibitions. Nevertheless, it is in this scenario, that they find paths across which no one has previously tread to alter a difficult reality; a change that seems like a mere mirage, a Fata Morgana[14] that the Bedouin society will never attain. Hanan's transcendent figure navigates the corridors of the children's ward in the hospital, persistently engaged in the challenging task of societal transformation. Meanwhile, Hiba's sharp as-pepper tongue, which accompanies brides and grooms on the eve of their matrimonial bond, is a space where there is room and value for each in the pair. Both women break barriers in a world of restrictions, passionately advocating for women within the inner courtyard rather than in the public sphere.

---

[14] *Fata Morgana* (Italian: [ˈfaːta morˈɡaːna]) is a complex form of superior mirage visible in a narrow band right above the horizon. The term *Fata Morgana* is the Italian translation of "Morgan the Fairy" (Morgan le Fay of Arthurian legend). These mirages are often seen in the Italian Strait of Messina, and were described as fairy castles in the air or false land conjured by her magic. [Wikipedia]

Hanan

On the Denial and Concealment of the Sexual Assault Phenomenon

Sometimes, I meet a person and something in my soul skips a beat, even if it's unclear exactly why or what intangible energy they transfer to me. I know that if I wait, pause for a moment, and listen closely, the answer to what I feel will come to me, even before I fully comprehend its meaning. Hanan was like that. Once, I heard a Bedouin doctor who worked in Hanan's department at the hospital speaking with a resident of her hometown. They spoke of Hanan with admiration, and according to what the person said, the entire community shared this sentiment. I heard in their voices a hint of that same wonder that came over me when I first met her. They had only one criticism of her: "She's Bedouin, but not exactly..." Once, they heard her speaking on the phone with her children. She spoke a different type of Arabic, the kind spoken by Arabs in the North. She isn't patronizing, yet still, she's "not exactly Bedouin" like the other women in the village. I believe she truly is different. Language is not just words and dialects. Sometimes, language is also an expression of one's inner world, personality, and the way a person behaves in life. Hanan is like that, and she's also Bedouin.

Hanan's Story

A Desert Home

My father was a Bedouin from the Negev, and my mother was born and raised in Ramla. My mother was orphaned at an early age. Her father, my grandfather, remarried another woman. In 1948, he fled with the entire family to Lebanon. My mother's older sister, who was already married, requested that the little girl, who was only seven years old at the time, remain with her. "She'll stay with me and my children until you return," the older daughter told her father, who was preoccupied with the journey he and his new family were about to undertake. The eldest daughter's offer to care for her younger sister seemingly eased his burden. The family never returned from Lebanon. My mother remained behind to grow up in her older sister's home, a sister who became like a mother to her.

My father worked as a plasterer in Central Israel. He was thirty when a matchmaker introduced him to my mother. She was already twenty-five at the time, which, in Bedouin culture, is considered late for marriage. My mother's family placed a single, firm condition on my father: they would only live in the central region, within the Lod-Ramla-Jaffa triangle. Back then, there was no permanent construction in the South, and the Bedouins lived in tents or shacks. Her family, especially her sister who raised her, wouldn't agree to my mother living "in some tent in the desert." My father kept his promise, and for fifteen years, they lived in Ramla.

My paternal grandfather owned fields and lands near Kibbutz Revivim. In 1948, the Army told him he needed to leave because they were going to use the area for drills and training. They relocated the family temporarily to an unrecognized village, and later, the government offered them land in Segev Shalom, where they could build their home in the new town. Those who had money bought plots and began to build. My father had already saved enough to purchase a land lot and construct a house. Two months after I was born, we moved to the Negev.

My mother had incredible financial awareness, despite never having attended school. Sometimes I think there are women with bachelor's and master's degrees who don't possess the kind of knowledge she did. The way she managed to save from the little money my father earned was nothing short of miraculous. For several years, we lived on financial assistance because my father was injured in a work accident, yet we lived relatively well compared to my uncles and cousins. Though my mother never had any formal education, she spoke fluent, beautiful Hebrew. Whenever we accompanied her to the clinic or hospital for an appointment, people would ask, "How does a Bedouin woman like you from Segev Shalom speak such lovely Hebrew?" She would answer, "First, I'm not Bedouin; and second, I learned from the market in Ramla and from our Jewish neighbors." She lived with her family in a mixed neighborhood of Arabs and Jews. When she went to the market, she'd hear a Jewish shopper say, "This pear is hard as a rock," and she'd ask him, "Why do you say like a 'rock'?" She understood that "rock" meant "hajar," and that the pear was very hard, like a rock. My mother said that's how she learned the words and accent to speak Hebrew fluidly.

I grew up in Segev Shalom and had trouble with the language dialect. My mother spoke a northern dialect of Arabic, while my family in Segev Shalom spoke a Bedouin southern dialect. As a child, when I ventured outside and spoke in my mother's dialect, the neighborhood kids would mock and laugh at me. But when I returned home and spoke in the Bedouin dialect, my mother would get angry. Over time, my six siblings and I learned to switch dialects in a split second, depending on whom we were addressing, and adjust our speech accordingly. In this way, we maintained both the northern dialect and the Bedouin dialect, like two languages side by side.

My mother was a strong woman. In Bedouin families, it's usually the father who is domineering and makes all the decisions. My mother wasn't controlling, but she was the dominant figure in our household. Ultimately, every decision came from her; every word she said had an impact, and every decision she made, we immediately embraced. We regarded her as a knowledgeable and wise woman, and my father did too. People loved her greatly in our family, as well as within our Bedouin community, despite the general dislike for foreign women. She was considered a "foreigner" because she was from the North, not Bedouin. When she arrived here forty years ago, in the 1970s, they didn't like non-Bedouin women and didn't welcome outsiders. But they loved, admired, and respected her, and often sought her advice. I vividly remember how relatives would come to her for guidance. For instance, if a women wanted to arrange a marriage for her daughter, she would come to my mother for advice: what to bring, what not to bring, what was appropriate, and what wasn't. They also consulted her regarding food because she introduced the community to a whole new variety of dishes, stuffed vegetables, and pickles they had never encountered before.

My mother entrusted me with her secrets. If she had an issue with one of the women in the family, she didn't like to confront her directly or share it with anyone else. Instead, she would confide in me, saying, "I've told you, and this is where it ends."

The Class Lawyer

In elementary and high school, the teachers would write our grades on the report card and add comments about each student. My report cards were filled with praise for my achievements, but there were always notes saying I was unruly and meddled in other people's affairs. The teachers were correct. I couldn't stand to see students being treated unfairly, getting hurt, mocked, or punished unjustly. I would fight for everyone without backing down, daring to stand up to the teachers and defend students who couldn't do it themselves.

My father never came to school. Even during elections, when everyone went to vote, he didn't show up. Only once, during the Gulf War, did he break his custom and went to the school to collect gas masks for us. My teacher recognized him and said, "You're Hanan's father? Hanan is such a smart, wonderful, clever girl — way to go for her! But she's the class lawyer. There's not a single time she doesn't jump in and meddle in things that aren't her concern." My father came home and angrily told me in the Bedouin dialect, "Your teacher says you're the class lawyer." Honestly, even what my father said didn't faze me. On the contrary, I liked the reason he was mad at me, and I insisted on continuing to be that way. But it bothered me that he said it in the Bedouin dialect as if he identified with the teacher and didn't see things from the inside, like in our family.

Just as I turned eighteen and finished high school, my uncle, a family doctor, opened his own private clinic and was looking for a secretary. I started working for him. I saw families bringing in their sick children and knew that this was where I wanted to be. I enrolled in a program at a nursing school, and from the very beginning, I felt like the hospital was my home. In the hospital, everyone is equal, regardless of whether they are Arab or Jewish, rich or poor, educated or simple folk. Everyone shares the same pain and the same worry in their eyes. I love interacting with people and the difference I can make, together with the team in the pediatric ward. The change isn't just in the child's health, but also in the feelings of the parents, who arrive panicked and leave calm and reassured.

"You Will Not Dictate Whom I Marry."

When I was nineteen, a boy I knew from high school wanted to marry me. My father opposed it, so did my mother, my uncles, and, in fact, the entire family was vehemently opposed. They said he was from a strange family that we didn't know. Strange? What did they mean by 'strange'? We all lived in the same area, but for a girl like Hanan — a smart girl who worked at the medical clinic and was now starting nursing school — she held a respected position, and we aren't going to marry her off to just anyone. For me, it wasn't a love story, and I didn't insist on marrying this young man, but the incident left a bitter taste, it seemed like a type of exploitation. Deep down, I said to myself, You won't decide for me. I'm not in love with this boy; I'm not fighting for him. But you won't decide whom I marry.

After a very short time, a boy from our family tried to get close to me. I loved his strong personality. He didn't conform to conventions or take everything for granted. He didn't have any higher education. He only finished high school and worked independently. He was handsome, spoke well, and was polite. For a year and a half, he tried to approach and talk to me. I was very tough — traditional and conservative. At first, we met at family events and talked, and gradually we began to speak on the phone. Then I told him, "Listen, my sister's daughter died from a hereditary kidney disease, and if I decide to marry you, I want us to get genetic tests before the wedding to see if we're even compatible, so we don't end up fighting for no reason." As soon as I said those words, I knew in my heart that I wanted to marry him.

I scheduled our separate appointments at the genetic clinic so no one would see us together. After two months, I received a letter saying that, like any other Bedouin couple in the South, neither of us carried the disease, and the likelihood of our children having genetic disorders was no higher than average for our population. Armed with this information, I went to my brother and told him I wanted to marry the young man, that we'd had tests done, and found no obstacles. When my brother returned home and told my parents, there was an explosion. My parents were furious about my initiative and the fact that I hadn't consulted them at all. My mother didn't like the boy or the idea that I was making my own decisions. For two and a half weeks, I'd say: "Good morning," but no one would answer. When I left for work, I'd say "Goodbye," and again, no one would respond.

The young man didn't give up. He came once, twice, three times, and even brought sheikhs from Jordan, relatives, and respected individuals to influence my father. In the end, he brought my family a *Jaha* — a group of distinguished people who come to show respect and ask for the bride's hand. My father had no choice but to agree. Father came back into the house and said to me, "This is what you wanted — you got it. May it bring you luck, good luck, to you." My mother cried all day. My uncle, the doctor, came and hugged her, saying, "You'll see that this man will stand by you more than your own sons." His prophecy and hope proved true. After the wedding, when my parents got to know him, they loved and admired him. They loved him until the very end. I don't regret for a single moment that I chose, insisted, and fought to marry him. He is the father of my six children. He supported me so much in pursuing my education, advancing my career, and learning to drive. Without him, I never would have driven a car. He took pride in me and told everyone, "My wife is a strong woman. My wife is knowledgeable, understanding, and knows how to speak well. I love going out with her and introducing her as my wife." It's not something to be taken for granted that a Bedouin man would express himself like that.

Women Give Birth Like Sheep

I completed my studies at nursing school when I already had my first baby and was pregnant with my second. I constantly sought to improve my skills, taking advanced courses in respiratory intensive care, neonatal care, and various pediatric specialties. Over the years,

I became the go-to confidante for both members of my husband's family and mine. Whenever they faced a problem, distress, or had a secret they couldn't share with anyone else, they turned to me. Sometimes, I feel overwhelmed. You know, when people come to you with things they don't want to share with anyone else, it weighs heavily on the heart. It's not just someone saying, "I have problems with my daughter-in-law," or, "I'm having issues with my husband." They come to confide in me when there's a serious illness in the family, when they're deciding whether to marry someone off or not, when there's been sexual assault or abuse. They come to share when something deeply troubling has happened.

After several years working in the pediatric department, I received a call from the regional administration, offering me a role overseeing the establishment of maternal and child health clinics in Bedouin villages. Naturally, I accepted the challenge. I loved the positive impact I had on families living in the Bedouin in the unrecognized villages. They would come to the clinics for medical care when their children were ill, but they had little awareness of vaccines, preventive care, or prenatal and postnatal monitoring. Many Bedouins didn't know what a maternal and child health clinic was and those who did weren't interested. I would meet the men at the clinics and speak to them, saying, "Your wife needs monitoring to ensure she's okay and that the baby is okay." The men would dismissively reply, "Our women have been giving birth like sheep their whole lives; they don't have a problem. My mother had fourteen children, and my wife had nine. What nonsense are you talking about?"

Following a year and a half of hard work, I began to see how these men, who had once spoken such harsh words, were now bringing their wives to the maternal and child health clinics, never missing an appointment. Slowly, they started bringing their babies for vaccinations. Sometimes I got angry with them; other times, I was gentle, explaining and encouraging them. Somehow, the importance of preventative medical care penetrated their awareness. Just as in high school, I couldn't sit quietly at the clinic when I saw a husband humiliating his wife in front of everyone. But this time, with a deeper understanding of the process that brings change, I didn't engage in head-on arguments with them. Instead, I led them to recognize the need to behave and speak differently. I approached each one through his own "door," as my mother used to say: "Every door has a key, and you need to find the right key."

When a Stone Falls Upon You

You asked me if I believe in Maktub (literally, "what is written," fate or destiny dictated by God). I told you that when a person falls into a well, they can choose to remain there, or they can decide to gather their strength and climb out. Maktub is akin to fate, but it's up to each person to choose how to cope with it. We've been talking for over an hour now, and I keep postponing the moment when I'll start telling you about the traumatic event that changed my life. What I've told you so far — about my family, studies, wedding, and work — has been a way of delaying sharing the painful story that I still carry with me to this day. But I am always grateful to God that I survived and that my daughter and I came out of it healthy and whole.

During the exam period in the second year of my master's in health systems management — a degree that many nurses pursue to advance their careers — we were renovating the house. I was extremely stressed, so I decided to head to Be'er Sheva to unwind a bit, do some shopping, and have lunch with a friend. I planned to return before the kids got back from school. Just as I sat down with my friend at a café, before we even touched our food, my husband called. He said he had received a phone call from his brother, who was shouting something about our daughter and the police. My husband couldn't figure out what had happened. I called my brother-in-law, and he said, "I need you to come right now to the Township Police Station near the Shoket Junction!"

"What happened? I'm in Be'er Sheva..." I said. "Something terrible has happened. I can't tell you over the phone. Your daughter is alive, but you need to come right now." I threw money on the table and bolted out of the restaurant. We hadn't touched a thing. The drive to Segev Shalom felt endless. The traffic light at the exit of Be'er Sheva is always slow, but this time, it felt especially sluggish. My friend was driving, and I told her I wanted to get out and run. She grabbed my hand and held onto me tightly to keep me from leaving the car.

I don't know how we made it. A guard stood at the entrance to the police station. I pushed past him and rushed inside. I saw the officer and shouted, "I want to see my daughter." The officer blocked my way. "What happened? Tell me, someone, please tell me what happened. I want to see my daughter!"

"Wait a second," the officer tried to stop me.

"I'm not waiting a single second!" I said, overwhelmed with emotion. The officer approached a heavy metal door and tried to open it. It was a door secured from the inside with a code. He called out to someone on the other side, but there was no answer. He knocked louder until an indifferent voice came from the other side, "What?"

"Your mother is about to faint, and you're not answering!" shouted the officer, who seemed visibly shaken by my panic. After what felt like an eternity, they brought my daughter out. I placed my hands on her face, on her body, to make sure she was okay. I hugged her tightly, and she started sobbing, trembling all over. "Mom, something terrible happened. I went back home from school to grab the sandwich I forgot and ran into someone in the house." I sensed she was afraid we might be angry with her. The only thing I told her was that she hadn't done anything wrong. I didn't even try to question her; or ask what happened. I knew something terrible had occurred, but at that moment, the most important thing was that I had my daughter back, safe and sound.

I held her, and soothed her like you calm a baby, "Mom is here, everything is fine. You behaved well, you didn't do anything wrong." I continued until she calmed down. The policewoman who escorted her told me they still don't know if there was rape, but it seems she was sexually assaulted. At that moment it felt as if the sky had fallen on me, like the ground had shifted beneath my feet. I didn't know how to function. I sat next to my daughter, hugged her tightly, and suddenly asked, "Tell me, did he take off your panties?"

I felt like I was falling into a deep, deep, deep, deep pit. And right there, in that profoundly deep pit, I seemed to hear a call from the heavens: "Be strong, you can deal with it." It was as if I had stepped into an icy shower that washed away all the filth. I felt God's presence. He won't abandon me, and I won't abandon my daughter.

A well-educated and unexpectedly empathetic, Bedouin investigative officer took me aside and said, "I completely understand you. I have three daughters at home, and I can truly feel the pain you're going through." He then added, "You have to listen and stay strong." I asked him if anyone knew about the incident. He replied, "No one knows, except for the uncle who brought her to the station. He came in, handed the girl to us, and began banging his head against the wall. I knew something terrible had happened. At first, there was no child investigator available, so we took some preliminary details from her until a professional investigator arrived along with an Arabic translator. Now your daughter needs to go to 'Soroka' as soon as possible to get checked to ascertain if she indeed suffered rape and to document exactly what she went through. We can't talk about it anymore so as not to disrupt the investigation.

They wanted to take us to the hospital in a police car, but I refused. She was just a fifth grader. "Why should she be put in a police car? Absolutely not. I have such a large family — what if someone sees us in the police car?" I called my husband, told him to come home immediately, and rush back to the house to get some clothes for my daughter. When I arrived, I saw the entire neighborhood swarming with police officers. They surrounded the house and wouldn't let me in. I told them I wanted to get some clothes for my daughter, but they refused to let me enter because they were waiting for a professional team to collect fingerprints. After arguing with them, they agreed on the condition that I wear gloves and not touch anything.

I was so distraught that I didn't even know which clothes to pack. A relative brought a new tracksuit. On the way, I called my husband and told him to stay home to meet our other kids when they got back from school. They couldn't come home to find the house in disarray, and we needed to be there to explain and reassure them. "Don't come with me to the hospital; I don't need you there. I'll handle this on my own. You need to be at home." I asked a family member to drive me and my daughter and followed the police car that was heading out to pick up the translator who lived near Omer. We then made our way to the hospital, and I could see the people in the ER staring at us with the police leading the way and us trailing behind. I asked the policewoman to keep her distance from me. "I speak Hebrew," I told her. "I don't want you standing by my side."

While my daughter was with the child investigator and the translator, I stayed outside with the social worker. We talked, and I felt her support. Meanwhile, my phone was blowing up with calls from my brother-in-law. He made me swear not to tell anyone in the family. Only my eldest daughter knew what had happened. The doctor who examined my daughter informed me there had been an assault, but no rape. I felt relieved and immediately called her uncle to tell him the results of the examination. Meanwhile, people started spreading rumors on WhatsApp: "A girl was raped in Segev Shalom". There were also rumors the girl had been stabbed and all sorts of stories. The entire neighborhood, the workmen who were there, everyone started running around looking for the guy who had harmed the girl.

When my daughter came out of her conversation with the investigator, I asked her if she wanted to talk about what had happened. She said she didn't want to speak. I suggested we come up with a different story, one that would be her story for life. It would be very similar to the real story but without mentioning the 'Eib)" (obscenity). 'Eib is a shameful sexual act that is forbidden to be done. When she told her uncle about the incident, she said, "He did something 'Eib to me." We agreed on this version of the narrative, which is entirely true except for the omission of the confrontation with the intruder inside. She truly did confront him, but there was an assault that we decided not to speak of at all — a sexual assault. That information never got out. To this day, even her father doesn't know what happened inside the house. My brother-in-law told my husband, "Tomorrow, you're going to slaughter three or four sheep and host a celebratory event where we invite everyone to come and share. We did it to announce that our daughter was healthy and unharmed, and to dispel all the rumors.

The school felt guilty for allowing the child to go back home to get the lunch she had forgotten without ensuring her parents were there. Two days after the incident, we slaughtered the sheep. The school principal came and blessed her, and her classmates made her a booklet with messages of support. Each student drew what they thought of her. In the drawings, there is a small thief, and my daughter is larger than life.

The Day After

In the first few days after the incident, my daughter was on a high, a kind of "euphoria." Everyone supported her, and she was the hero of the day. But a few weeks later, she crashed. She began sleeping a lot, having nightmares, she'd clutch the Quran and place it under her pillow. She became aggressive, stubborn, and irritable, and started obsessively keeping everything neat and clean. Anything out of place bothered her. She wanted to keep everything spotless and organized. Suddenly, she took responsibility for the laundry, folding it as meticulously as they do in stores. If anyone took out a shirt, even her father, she'd get upset. She also insisted on bathing her younger siblings every night, even though in winter, I usually bathed them every other day. That's when I realized my daughter needed psychological help.

My husband opposed therapy. He couldn't understand how mere conversations with our daughter could help her. He thought they might even cause more harm. I didn't want to involve the social worker from the welfare authorities and risk having a file opened on her. So, I reached out to a Hebrew-speaking psychologist, because I knew my daughter could easily express herself in Hebrew. I also understood she wanted to keep what had happened a secret, and speaking in Hebrew would reduce the risk of anyone close finding out. We began traveling to Be'er Sheva every Tuesday. Each session cost me 250 shekels. My husband mocked me, saying, "You're wasting your money and doing something foolish." Every time I took her to the psychologist, he suggested I take her to a sheikh. "He'll take the Quran, and this will pass," he said. I told him, "Fine, go ahead and take her. But I'm going to keep taking her to the psychologist because it's helping her. I can see it's doing her good; she's improving." He never took our daughter to the sheikh, and I kept driving her to the psychologist. I felt she needed support and treatment. At school, she had a wonderful homeroom teacher who stood by us. He didn't know exactly what had happened, but he had heard about an incident involving a thief and violence. I salute her homeroom teacher. I wrote him a thank-you letter and sent it to the Director General of the Ministry of Education. For a person like that, I take off my hat.

A girl or young woman who has been assaulted is entitled to support and assistance from the state at the "Inbal" Center for the Treatment of Sexual Assault Victims. However, a year and a half had already passed by the time we received government subsidies for treatment at the "Inbal" Center. I struggled to keep paying privately every week, because the cost was so high. I'm a mother of six, I work, and my husband is self-employed — sometimes he has work, sometimes he doesn't. After a year and a half, when we became eligible for the "Inbal" Center, we switched to treatment there. To my surprise, there was a female Arab psychologist from the north, fluent in Arabic, there to greet us. My daughter felt at ease with her but refused to open up about the incident. She attended the sessions and spent her time playing, coloring, doing crafts, and having fun — but she didn't want to talk about that one thing she was supposed to be there to discuss. When we returned home, she would be irritable as if sending me a message: she didn't want to go back to a place where people talked about what hurt her. Two years after the incident, she told me, "I'm not going back to therapy." I couldn't force her. Since then, I've been her only caregiver. She hardly talks about what happened, but the signs and scars remain, etched in her soul.

At the peak of my emotional crisis, when I felt suffocated and drained, I discovered my husband was talking to some girl on the phone. I found out by chance. I thought to myself, "Wow... at a time when I'm in distress and facing a family crisis like this, and he knows what we're going through, he's out there fantasizing?" Even if it's just phone calls, it was a source of deep pain for me. I went to the dean's office at the university, told them I'd been through a family trauma, and asked for help. They arranged for me to see a psychologist at the university. I went to the sessions, and it was the first time in my life that I cried in front of someone. After two meetings, the psychologist told me, "You must share this with someone in your family." She asked if my mother knew what had happened. I said, "My mother doesn't know. I'm not going to do that to her. Why would I bring my mother pain?"

"And does your sister know?"

I told her that my sister didn't know either. She's two years older than me, but I've always been the one supporting her, not the other way around. People often assume I'm the older one, and she's younger. My sister has always been quiet and gentle, accepting everything she's given and every social norm without question. She even got married this way — they arranged a match for her, and she went along with it. With all her problems, she turns to me, and I solve them. Now I'm supposed to go to her and burden her with my troubles? The psychologist looked at me and said, "You only think about others and never about yourself. If you don't share this with someone in your family, it will sit on your heart like a stone. You have to let it out."

I decided to confide in one of my husband's sisters. Later on, I chose to share with my sister, as well. To my surprise, she said, "Hanan, from the first day it happened, I knew your daughter had been sexually assaulted. I felt your pain deep inside and sensed your distress. I could see how awful you looked and how terrible you felt, without you saying a single word. But I chose not to speak up until you were ready." It was like a weight had been lifted off my shoulders.

Eventually, I sat down for an honest conversation with my husband. He admitted that he wanted to escape the harsh reality we were living in and that he felt like he was in a different world when he spoke on the phone to that girl — a girl he had never even met in person. Someone had given him her phone number. "I miss you," he told me. "You were at the hospital, at school, and most of all, most of all with our daughter." I looked him in the eye and said, "She's not just my daughter from a previous marriage. She's your daughter too."

My husband isn't a bad man or a bad father. In Bedouin society, people simply don't understand anything about handling sexual assault. And really, how can anyone grasp a subject that is outright denied and brushed aside with, "In our community, this doesn't happen. We're a religious, conservative, devout society with strong family ties. This doesn't happen to us!" I knew I was facing a tough and even dangerous task. I understood that change could only grow from the pain in my heart. But before I tell you more about that, I want to address one important matter and talk about the punishment of the offender.

The attacker was arrested. He was an illegal resident, a man from the territories who was familiar with our neighborhood. He knew our house was under renovation and probably knew where we kept the key. He unlocked the door and went inside. When my daughter came in, he bumped into her. My daughter described him perfectly — she's a smart girl. When they showed me the sketch the police had drawn based on her description and then showed me his real photo, I swear to you, it looked like someone had sat right in front of him and sketched it. She gave a complete description. He was caught and imprisoned. I didn't miss a single court session. I attended every single court hearing, even the ones conducted in the middle of my work shift. It was a closed court session because she was a minor; so, there was no one else inside. I stared directly at him, and he couldn't lift his eyes to meet mine. In court, when I took the stand, I didn't cry. But even though I was so strong, my voice trembled a little as I repeated the words she had told me about what he did to her.

The court proceedings were conducted entirely in Hebrew. They did provide him with a translator, but everything was in Hebrew. I remember everyone listening to my testimony, not just the judge and the lawyers but even the stenographer and the guard standing by the door. When I finished, they started asking me personal questions: "Where do you work?" "What do you do?" "Where do you live?" "Where are you from?" "Are you really from that family?" One of the prosecutors later told me that my testimony had a significant impact on the judge.

The attacker was sentenced to ten years in prison. On the day of the verdict, the prosecutor told me it was a precedent and that they would certainly appeal. And indeed, they appealed to the Supreme Court. The appeal was rejected, and he's still in prison. At first, he pretended to be mentally ill and was hospitalized in a psychiatric facility. He even tried to escape. His family attempted to get a report from an Arabic-speaking doctor claiming he was mentally ill, but the court appointed a psychiatrist who determined that he wasn't ill, just faking it. If he hadn't gone to prison, I would have lost my mind. His imprisonment and ten-year sentence brought closure to my daughter. She feels safe. She feels like there is justice in the world. I couldn't have let things happen any other way and have my daughter believe there's no justice in this world.

It pains me deeply that this tragedy happened, but in our faith, we always say that even in something bad, there's something good hidden. One must find the good in everything. We were fortunate that the man came from outside. If it had been someone from the family, there would have been murder, or they would have married the girl off to her rapist — which is unthinkable and has to change. Today, my daughter is much stronger, and wiser, and understands that while there are dangers in life, we will always be there for her. But I believe that's not enough. When I ask myself why this happened to our family, why it happened to me, I think there's no such thing as coincidence. I have the strength to make a difference not only in the children's ward at the hospital, but also in the most painful and afflicted corners of our society, where people are so ashamed that they prefer other, traditional solutions that only harm the victim further.

"Fighting to Ensure that Rays of Light Can Also Shine into Our Society"

At my lowest point, I realized that Bedouin society desperately needed to change its attitude toward sexual assault. I began collecting articles and reading about sexual and sexual harassment in Bedouin society. I was surprised by the new information I discovered — particularly how the research literature acknowledged the problem even though it remains hidden, with no one willing to recognize its existence. When the state enacted the Sexual Harassment Prevention Law, it didn't take our culture into account, nor did it make the effort to understand what sexual harassment means to us. Only examples of harassment in Jewish society were provided. No one spoke of the harassment or assault occurring within traditional, patriarchal, closed society that doesn't acknowledge the issue at all.

In the past, there was a traditional Bedouin tribal court. If a young man sexually harassed or assaulted a Bedouin girl, he was severely punished. However, what girl and which family would sacrifice themselves, their daughter, and all the daughters of the tribe just to punish the young man? Usually, families keep the assault hidden and remained silent on the matter. We have to bring abuse and harassment to light, put it on the agenda, and talk about it — not deny its existence and pretend it's not there.

When I talk about the issue of sexual assault and harassment with educated Bedouins, meaning, those with bachelor's and master's degrees, they get angry and attack me: "You're speaking nonsense; you're tarnishing our good name. What are you talking about? Who told you there's sexual harassment?" I can't tell them my daughter was sexually assaulted, but I describe the data I've collected from the welfare authority, social workers, and doctors. It's all confidential and secret, but it's there. There are statistics, there are numbers, and even if they're incomplete, they indicate a severe problem where the victim remains in the shadows and often faces additional punishing social consequences from the community. I tell them about women who were raped and reported it to the welfare office, only to be told that they must file a police report. Then they disappear and never speak about it again. The woman doesn't want to involve the police. All she wants is help and treatment. She seeks support, but she doesn't receive it from the welfare authority because they have to follow state protocols — report to the police and open a file. The woman has to go to the police station, and someone sees her entering and immediately asks, "What are you doing there? It's a police station; women don't just walk into a police station. What happened?" — but she wants to keep what happened to her a secret, quietly hidden away.

If a girl dares to step into a police station and says, "I've been raped," "I've been sexually assaulted within my family," or "I've been sexually assaulted at work," the police immediately look for a sheikh to take her under his protection. The police mean well — they want to protect the girl from being executed for dishonoring her family. But they are also reluctant to apprehend the boy and get entangled with either the girl's tribe or the tribe of the boy. Sometimes they smuggle the girl to a shelter or place her under the protection of a sheikh who tries to mediate between her family and the family of the boy, ultimately arranging a marriage between them. But that's not how it should be. Why should she have to marry her rapist? No matter where you go, you'll always hear that it's her fault and that the victim is to blame. As a law enforcement body, the police don't know how to handle the situation properly. At the welfare authority, a Bedouin social worker tells me, "I understand she needs help and treatment, but I can't do anything to aid her without opening a police file." In my case, when I called the police officer and told him I needed to meet with him in person because there was a leak of information and WhatsApp messages were spreading throughout the town that a girl had been raped, he received me immediately. But when I wanted to interview him about the issue of sexual abuse and harassment, he suddenly refused to see me.

Today, I volunteer for an organization that aids women who have been sexually assaulted. We support women who reach the welfare authority but don't want to take the matter to the police. We have agreements with welfare offices outside the Bedouin communities and can refer them to psychologists specializing in sexual assault. The organization itself engages in many activities, such as diagnosing children with learning disabilities and intellectual impairments, but I only volunteer in the field of sexual assault care. Running an organization is a big task: budgeting, fundraising, and recruiting professionals. The university hosted a large conference on Bedouin society, attended by mayors and council heads from Bedouin cities and towns. I presented the initiative to address sexual harassment. The poster on display included verses from the Quran. They photographed our council head next to the poster, so he can no longer claim he's never heard of sexual harassment in Bedouin society. During the ceremony, he declared his intention to promote women's welfare and address their issues, but in reality, nothing happened afterward.

I always strive to lead, but it's challenging. My work in the children's ward takes up much of my time. I still work almost full-time, and I'm also a mother of six, including a one-year-old baby. But

I'll be honest: the hardest aspect of this struggle is realizing that our society isn't ready to face this issue. I don't feel like I've done enough, but at least I know I didn't sit idly by or accept what happened to my daughter. I refuse to remain silent about any case I come across in my life. It's probably in my nature to seek justice. The teachers at school were right when they wrote in my report card that I don't sit quietly when others are harmed. I saved my daughter, but what will happen to other girls? What will happen to young women who are abused and are subjected to force against their will?

I am a warrior for awareness in Bedouin society, fighting for the proper treatment of sexual harassment victims. But above all, I am Bedouin. Being the daughter of a Bedouin father and a mother from the center of the country means understanding the thoughts and beliefs of the South, but also knowing that things can be different. So, I fight to ensure that rays of light can also shine into our society.

Hiba

A Local Initiative

I initially attributed Hiba's exuberant joy and warmth to the news of her upcoming marriage. Later, I thought it might be tied to the early days of building her new family and her pregnancy, which quickly followed. Hiba was part of a group of fellows seeking to bring about social change in the Negev. Slowly but surely, the group members began to explore ways to turn what once seemed like distant dreams into reality. These were the first buds of new ideas, mixed with hesitation, a sense of responsibility, and the barriers that constantly stand in the way of those who try to change reality with all its complexities and constraints. Such challenges are usually daunting because of the unknown, the murky, and the feeling of a lack of firm footing. To ease the distress of the participants, we held personalized guidance sessions with each fellow in the program.

The project Hiba chose was to establish a neighborhood community activity center, a kind of local recreation center. She lived in a neighborhood far from the nearest community center, and because of the distance, the residents couldn't participate in its activities. It quickly became clear to me that for Hiba, planning and action worked side by side. She identified an unused public building in her neighborhood, enlisted her entire family to help clean it up and collect whatever equipment they could find, and set up a network of classes for the neighborhood children, charging only a symbolic fee. Hiba knew nothing about the organizational structure of Israel's Community Center network, its budgets, the multi-stage appointment process, or its institutionalized methods. Yet, as a single, independent woman with initiative, charisma, and influence over the entire neighborhood, she managed to create a magnificent "mini community recreation center" that thrived.

As Hiba neared the end of her studies in the leadership program, I suggested she enroll in a master's program at the college. At the time, Hiba was in the early stages of her second pregnancy, but she laughed and said that a child is a blessing and beginning M.A. studies wouldn't be an issue for her. I didn't teach in her program, so I would occasionally meet her only on the college steps, both of us hurrying off to our tasks. One day, as she was finishing her studies, I stopped her and asked where she was headed. There, on the steps, I heard for the first time about her new initiative: preparing brides and grooms for "Laylat Al-Dakhle," the wedding night.

Hiba's Story

A Family Photo

I am Hiba Abu Amar Al-Sayyid. With all due respect to my husband and the Abu Amar family, my name is Al-Said, my father's family name. They are my original family, and I lived with them for twenty-three years. I was born into a family blessed with fourteen children. We originally lived in Lod, and all the children went to school there. But as we got a little older, my father noticed that the local teenagers were getting into drugs. Fearing for his sons, he decided to move to the Negev. I'm the eleventh child in the family and the first born in Rahat. All my siblings are educated: we have a doctor, a lawyer, an engineer, and teachers. My older sisters couldn't continue their studies because society pressured my father to keep them at home. By the time I wanted to study, my father didn't mind anymore, perhaps because times had changed a bit.

My father worked in renovations. Most of the time, he worked as a plasterer, but he could handle other construction jobs as well. My mother wasn't educated, but she had her unique wisdom shaped by her life experience. Whenever someone in the neighborhood was in trouble or wanted to do something special, they'd tell them to go and talk to her: "Do it like Rada!" My mother is the perfect example of someone who knows how to navigate difficult circumstances without ever giving up. She would bring clothes, gold, and rings from various places and sell them to women. Her parents had olive trees, so she'd collect the olives, make oil, and sell that too. She could stand up to anyone but always remained positive. She's my guiding light, my role model in life.

I am the most quiet and disciplined student. Even in elementary school, I remembered every word my teachers said. I absorb wisdom and put it into practice. Even when I lied, people believed me — I don't know why. Once, in sixth grade, a teacher told me, "Hiba, always look at yourself as if you're on the outside. Critique yourself before others critique you. Give yourself feedback before it comes from others — that's how you'll succeed." I always remember those words when I feel stressed or find myself in a conflict. I remember his advice, step out of the picture, and observe myself from the outside. That's when I find the answer and formulate my response.

In elementary and middle school, I was a silent student. I sat at the back of the classroom and didn't speak. I always received excellent grades in written expression. I was the sweet, unobtrusive student, who never caused trouble or harmed anyone. It wasn't until tenth grade that my life truly began. Suddenly, I found the courage to speak up and stand my ground, and I realized the earth wouldn't crumble beneath me. I began thinking of others and volunteering for everyone as if I had finally emerged from my shell. I can't explain what changed in me.

Until 7th grade, I tended to my family's goat herd. I was responsible for over twenty goats. In 7th grade, my mother changed my role and asked me to work at home so that she could teach me how to be a homemaker. I took over responsibility for cleaning, cooking, and preparing pita bread every day before heading off to school. In the evening, I would prepare the dough, and at five in the morning when my father woke up to pray, he would wake me so I could bake. In the early in the morning, I would make 50 or 60 pita breads. This became my daily routine from seventh grade until my third year of college. I bought my backpack and half of my supplies with the money I earned from various jobs. I wanted to feel independent.

When I finished high school, I signed up for a degree in social work. But my brother, a lawyer, intervened: "You can study, but not social work. You're going to take all the women to a shelter? Forget it!" Regretfully, I had to give it up. Instead, I turned to special education, finding solace in the knowledge that I could still help people there.

While at college, I was active in the student association. I always served as the students' representative and even received an letter of appointment from the mayor, naming me as the first student representative at City Hall. I often found myself the only woman in a room full of men — high school principals, heads of education and culture in the municipality, and the mayor. It was a bit challenging because the meetings were held in the evening, and I found it difficult to go out at 7 p.m. to the community recreation center and sit among men. My brother would pick me up, chiding me,

"What, are you crazy? There are no girls there. It's not respectable for you to go." Disheartened, I gave up and left. Later, I began working at "AJEEC," an Arab-Jewish organization dedicated to developing Bedouin society. I worked as a project coordinator for programs related to girls in distress. I listened to all their secrets and the mistakes they had made in their lives, and it was far from easy. During this period, I learned a great deal about life and realized that a woman must never give up or lower her head before a man. I'm not a feminist; I'm a devout woman who follows Allah's commandments. But nowhere is it written that a woman should be treated like a doormat.

At times, I took risks, especially when returning home from college and either my brother or someone else from the family was late to pick me up from the station. I would stand there, surrounded by a throng of criminals and other uncultured individuals who lingered attempting to strike up a conversation, or those who would fling their door open and curtly call over to me, "Come on, get in." I was afraid of being raped, though I don't know why. My mother used to tell me every day that she would never forgive me if it happened. Instead of greeting me with a warm good morning, she offered a stern warning, "If you do something bad, we'll know everything." At the time, I perceived her words as a threat. Only now do I understand what she said as her clumsy way of saying "Take care of yourself," but in harsher words.

I cherish my home, and my parents, and I love being somewhat on the sidelines, observing the ebb and flow of people around me. Sometimes, I venture out on either an errand, perhaps to the city center, a clinic, or a meeting, without a ride, yet I'm not the least bit anxious. I sit quietly to the side and wait. During these moments, I revel in watching others, taking pleasure in witnessing what unfolds around me. I adore being on the periphery, viewing the whole scene: observing what's happening, what's changed. When I sit there, set apart and observing, I see many things as if for the first time.

Spicy Pepper

From our sprawling family tree, I was one of the last to marry. Growing up, I observed the perennial problems that often besiege marriages, and perpetual misunderstandings, which sometimes even culminate in divorce. Invariably, it was the woman who bore the brunt, left with scarce opportunities. The odds of starting a good life following a divorce appeared minuscule, feeling like one in a hundred. It's the woman who bore the weight of continuing life steeped in suffering and hardship. This reality suffocated me as if it were my responsibility to effect a change. I told myself that I needed to guide the young women I worked with before they embarked on their new life chapter — whether picturesque or perilous. Unbeknownst to me at the time, this was called "coaching", but I firmly believed that everyone is able to learn and improve. My dream was to manage something significant. I began instructing these girls to be strong, or as they say in Arabic, "pepper." What does that mean? It means being independent, being everything by yourself, not needing anyone else. Once, a Jewish taxi driver told me, "You're not just any pepper, you're a spicy pepper, like fiery harissa." It's not that collaboration isn't necessary, but when you are a homemaker, you are essentially everything. Especially when you are a mother, you are everything. I speak as a conservative woman, Arab, Muslim. I am not a sheikh, as I do not have a familiarity with the entire Quran.

I strive to do everything in my power to ensure that God is pleased with me. When it comes to relationships with men, I always say, "Respect yourself. If you put yourself at the center, everything will develop well, everything will be blessed. If you are not at the center, you will not succeed. If you don't give to yourself, you cannot give to others. Start with yourself; begin by respecting your mind and listening to your heart."

My husband is not from my close family. During my first year as a teacher, he worked as a book salesman in a store across the street from the school. He harbored feelings for me for two long years without my knowledge. He discreetly sought me out and asked others about me, yet I was completely unaware. Eventually, he sent someone to speak with me. Initially, I rebuffed the idea and stated that I hadn't considered such matters. I explained to the messenger that my mind was preoccupied with my studies, and that I have brothers with whom such topics should be discussed. I felt somewhat embarrassed to converse about this subject, with an outsider, a relative of his, although I did know the man who approached me. Months passed, and he asked me again if I would agree to meet him. I directed him to my brothers. He chose to see my brother, the lawyer. My brother asked him if he knew me well. He replied that he had seen me occasionally but confessed that he did not know me intimately. To our astonishment, my brother, the traditional, conservative lawyer, surprised us by saying, "Times have changed, it's not like before. She has a phone, and you two need to speak to each other directly." And so, this lawyer had changed.

My brother came home and told me that someone had approached him inquiring about me. He wasn't too fond of the man's spiky hairstyle, but he found him to be a nice, decent fellow and had given him my number so he could contact me. Two days later, that man called, and we spoke on three consecutive days. At the end of our conversations, I agreed that he could take the next step. Two weeks later, he came to my house with his parents in tow. Three months flew by in a whirlwind of secret meetings and whispered plans, culminating in our engagement and swiftly followed by our wedding. We had a wonderful, secret engagement, marked by clandestine dinners at restaurants where no one knew us. Once, I pretended to run errands with my nieces, only to drop them off at a convenient location while we slipped away to dine alone, savoring our moments of rebellion. We really lived it up. In my conservative family, even with a wedding on the horizon, just three months down the road, sitting together in the living room with the door closed was forbidden. When I was young, I was always strategically seated between my sisters when their fiancés visited. They would send me to see what they were talking about, to monitor what they were doing. And yet, ironically, I was the one who dared to break the rules. Once, we even stayed out together at a restaurant until one in the morning.

When I married my husband, they informed me that in his family, everyone wanted a second wife, as it is their custom. I won't pretend I wasn't afraid. To this day, I harbor fears, though I reveal them to no one. My father-in-law is the sole member of his family who refrained from this practice, but now, at the age of seventy, he suddenly considers the choice seriously. This aggravates me and harms us as a family, especially his sons. Why, after all these years, does he entertain such thoughts? Because if he has children with a second wife, we will be responsible for her. We are a tight-knit family, and we do not want another burden, another task, another challenge for our family to navigate. In Islam, it is permitted if a man wants children, and his wife has not borne him any. That is the reasoning I can accept.

Until now, my husband has had no reason to desire a second wife. He has children, and he has food — I am a culinary artist, crafting exquisite dining experiences for him. At home, I truly pamper him. When he leaves, and later returns at night from the Shig, he finds dried fruits, tea, and freshly squeezed juice waiting for him. He has everything. I await him with respect and joy, and the children are already asleep. Sometimes, I even prepare various little surprises for him. I create an atmosphere filled with excitement, so he will feel he lacks for nothing.

If one day my husband decides he wants another wife, it will be difficult. I don't want to exhaust my nerves and energy worrying about this possibility. I wish to live my life moment by moment. Dwelling on such thoughts might just damage our lives. If the moment of truth arrives, I truly don't know what I'll do. Thus, I've resolved not to waste a minute of my energy pondering negative outcomes. I refuse to entertain the thought, not wanting to invoke the law of attraction to bring this problem closer. I am here and he is here, so that's that. Let us live in the present. However, believe me, a woman is wise if she has her faith, her belief in God, and her trust in the Quran. If asked whether it's better for a husband to visit prostitutes or to take a second wife, I would say he should take a second wife to avoid bringing home diseases — AIDS and other sexually transmitted diseases — and social disgrace. In the North, they claim not to have second wives, yet infidelities abound, and many visit brothels. Once, a female teacher said, "I wish my husband would just marry a second wife and not visit prostitutes." It's more peaceful that way. True, it's hard at first, but it's ultimately more serene. A second wife is preferable to disease and disgrace. If there's a second wife, and still he respects you, I remain neutral, neither condemning nor condoning. If he has his reasons and can support two women in two households, I won't object.

Steering Her Life

I passed my driving theory test on the first attempt during my senior year in high school. There was a free course offered at school, I seized the opportunity and passed with flying colors. After graduation, I was eager to take driving lessons. However, my brother, who had just returned from studying law in Russia, firmly objected. He confronted me, asking, "Why the sudden urge to learn now? And, why of all places, learn to drive in Be'er Sheva? Just sit quietly. I don't agree that girls should learn to drive," he said. I told him that our father was still alive, and therefore, he, my brother, did not get to decide what I was allowed to do with my life. He, acting as the lawyer, insisted that I should not learn to drive and even clashed with our father about it. My father told him, "I am here, so you will not decide for me. If I die, then you can make decisions." My mother didn't want to get involved and said I needed to reach agreement with my brothers. Essentially, she supported my desire to learn to drive, but she was more concerned about avoiding family disputes. I decided to drop the matter, which was a wise decision. During my brother's internship in Ashkelon — for which he left early in the morning and returned in the evening — I managed to sneak off to Be'er Sheva to take driving lessons and make it back home within an hour and a half, all without any supervision. I passed my driving test on the third try. Afterward, I didn't drive due to the fear of getting a flat tire and not knowing whom to call for help in the middle of the road. Due to overwhelming fear, I didn't touch the steering wheel for seven years. All that time, I knew that driving was the path of independence — a means to go wherever I wished, without anyone knowing. Only by driving could you truly steer the course of your own life.

Before getting married, I dreamed of owning a car, and even diligently saved money to make it a reality. But when I got engaged, my brother insisted it wouldn't look right for me to buy a car when my fiancé didn't have one. He said it would be embarrassing for people to say, "He's using her car." So, I set my savings aside. Two months after the wedding, we bought a car together, with my husband contributing a bit as well. I was a new driver, as it was the first time I drove. I didn't have a "New Driver" sign hanging in my car window, but in essence, I was a new driver. In my husband's neighborhood, women weren't allowed to drive. Even his brother's wife, who had a license, never took the wheel. At first, I only took the car out for time-sensitive commitments — visits to my parents, catching up with friends, or running errands in the center of Rahat. But after three years, I took the car everywhere. I am my own driver. My husband does not chauffeur me around. I drive myself to visit my parents. When I was seen confidently maneuvering my car everywhere through the streets, slowly the neighborhood transformed. Now, almost all the women drive, and nearly every household maintains a car for the women.

When a woman drives, it can indeed cause some friction in a marriage. My husband and I drifted apart because of the car. I live my life independently; he's not involved with the children's appointments at the health clinic, or anything related to kindergarten, or school. I don't need a husband to sit beside me, pretending to be the driver. This arrangement suits me better, but it has truly distanced us from each other. I even conducted my own personal research and realized that the car is one of the key reasons for marital problems — leading to the prospect of a second wife, a growing distance between husband and wife, or even divorce. The car allows a woman to manage life on her own — her husband isn't involved, doesn't cooperate, and remains clueless about her life. He doesn't know where she goes, or how she spends money. Her husband doesn't visit her parents and is unaware of who her friends are — he's simply not in the picture. Getting a driver's license is akin to Independence Day for a woman.

The Wedding Night- "Aduhla Night"

Among the Bedouins, mothers do not prepare their daughters before marriage, feeling too ashamed to discuss such matters. Sometimes, the bride hears from her older sisters or married friends that eventually, in time, everything will settle and gradually fall into place. Women are given the impression that they are secondary; it's the man that matters. Sex is an incredibly sensitive subject in our culture. Girls are constantly told, "It's forbidden, forbidden, forbidden, it's

'Eib." 'Eib ... 'Eib means it's absolutely prohibited and shameful. It's taboo to even mention — this is our societal code. I always feared rape. But rape isn't only physical; it's like stealing or shattering your dreams, suffocating your spirit. There are girls and young women who excelled in their studies and then they were raped — not by strangers, but by being married off too early their dreams were stolen. No one told the men, "Marry her on the condition that she continues her education." These girls could have become doctors. Isn't it a tragedy? Instead, they trained to become kindergarten assistants. That is a form of coercion or rape! Some women were kind-hearted and dutiful, yet their lives were stolen and utterly destroyed. They didn't just stand still; they were forced backward, all because of the wedding night.

For most women, the wedding night is less of a celebration and more a night of curses. Typically, young brides have no intimate experience whatsoever. Contrary to popular belief, most boys are also inexperienced. There are honorable young men preserve their innocence — though some succumb to social pressure, curiosity, or an inner restlessness and experiment earlier. But generally, even men lack experience in this realm. Technology and the internet expose them to a certain "boldness" or "insolence," often mistaken for openness or honesty. In our time, discussing such matters was shrouded in shame, but today, that veil has lifted. Nevertheless, guidance remains essential. She needs it, and so does he. In truth, he might need it even more.

I decided that the situation needed to change. I resolved to prepare brides for married life and for what transpires between them and their husbands on the wedding night. I realized it wasn't enough to prepare the brides alone; the grooms needed preparation, as well. Intimacy is a shared experience, and each spouse has a role in what will happen. I began reading books and learning how to guide both brides and grooms. At first, I would visit the bride during the week of the wedding, even if I didn't know her beforehand. The house would be bustling with women, all eager to help. I would sit and talk with the bride, gently bringing up the delicate subject of intimacy, preparing her for the night ahead.

I feigned shyness, especially when broaching intimate subjects between husband and wife. I would cover my face with a scarf, as if embarrassed to speak of such topics. Inevitably, the bride's mother or sister would call me into the kitchen and say, "Thank you, don't be shy, please continue." Soon, others began to take notice. Another woman who had been present would call me later and say, "Please, come and guide my daughter, but don't let her know it was my idea." And that's how word of my discreet counsel spread quietly, by word of mouth.

It's a secret, yet not a secret. I don't need to announce my advice over a microphone. I tell the bride-to-be how she should be with her husband on their wedding night. I give her a wrapped book that contains bridal guidance. Sometimes, I quote a verse from the Quran and explain its meaning, reinforcing what I am teaching her. For instance, I describe how beautiful life will be once the wedding night is over. At the wedding ceremony, I sit beside her chair and whisper, "This is your night. It's a joyous occasion, something wonderful. He chose you; his parents chose you. This is truly the most beautiful day of your life." I also encourage her, saying, "You look so stunning, more beautiful than other brides," because I want her to feel confident and strengthened.

When the food arrives, I start joking with her about how delicious it is, but that what awaits her tonight is just as delightful. It's my little bit of "craziness," but she laughs. I tell her, "You should be like a cute cat with him, a delightful white cat, but remain a strong woman. Don't just be like the bed sheet. Enjoy yourself. It's not just for him, it's for you too. You are an integral part of this experience. Do you know what a prostitute is? Forget those boundaries. But also, you need to enjoy it — you're not a prostitute. Be like one in the sense that you give your body but enjoy it. Wear something short. Don't care. This is your day too, not just his. Sex is delightful; it does something wonderful — it cools your body, it cools your soul, trust me. Afterward, you'll even look at yourself differently. You'll see that you love yourself. After each encounter between you, look in the mirror: you'll see yourself as if you've just had an exfoliation, a massage, or a facial treatment. It will give you a different feeling. It's something beautiful, but it also has its rules."

Now I get into the delicate, difficult part. There are boundaries and rules to this game. We enjoy the game, but while you make it your own, there are still rules you must follow. The rules are to respect yourself as a person — dignified and mature, capable of enjoying herself. When I say this, the brides-to-be fall silent, their eyes fixed on me, eager to hear more. Even the boldest bride remains quiet and does not question. She just listens and watches. Even if someone calls them aside, they don't want to hear from anyone else but me. I tell her, "Enjoy yourself; this is your night. It's your privilege, your prerogative, your right — but remember, we come from a conservative society. If your husband believes you've had past experience and already know how to behave with a man in bed, it will likely cause serious problems. Since I read books, there were times I had more knowledge than my husband about what to do in bed — but I never let him realize that. I played dumb and went along slowly. Why? Because if a woman seems more knowledgeable than a man, it can diminish his confidence. Be careful not to give your husband the impression that you have past experiences, or that you're too familiar with intimacy. Men often like to feel they are in control in bed. That's true for men everywhere, not just in our community. The man wants to be the lion, and that you are his lioness. Let him be the lion, but don't forget yourself, and remember that you have your rights and needs too.

There is another rule, another crucial point to consider. I gently explain to her that she is not obligated to go through with consummating the marriage that night: "Today you got married, today was the celebration, but the Aduhala night (wedding night) doesn't necessarily have to be tonight. It can happen tomorrow or the day after, if you are not emotionally ready or if your body is too weary. After a week of intense preparations, it's perfectly acceptable for you to wait."

Afterward, I make my way to the groom's side. They look at me in awe and say, "How strong you are, aren't you embarrassed?" "Embarrassed?" Why be embarrassed? I speak to the groom from wisdom, "Be gentle with your wife. She is yours not just for tonight, but for your whole life. Be kind and considerate. There's no rush; there's always tomorrow, the day after, or even next month. Treat her with the respect she deserves because she is your wife." I remind him not to be harsh with her, emphasizing that she is his other half, not a prostitute. When I say this, they look at me, stunned. I know how to convey this delicately, using our expressions. I also show them where the importance of treating your wife properly is written in the Quran. I tell the men, "Don't make it rough. You know what I mean. Be sensitive! She might experience bleeding; don't react with shame! Have you heard of women being taken away in an ambulance? Isn't that disgraceful? Be a little tender, even though you are a man." I speak using such language. I am not embarrassed to talk about intimacy, but I pretend to be a bit emotional so that my words touch their hearts.

I write the grooms a blessing, a warm, encouraging note, and give it to them. I tell them what to do the night before they are together with their wife on their wedding night: first, take a shower, here's what you should eat, and what you shouldn't eat, this is what might bother you. Sometimes, I go to their home and create a romantic atmosphere with candles to cast a soft, warm glow, arrange an array of flowers on the bed, and spritz perfume to fill the room with delicate fragrance. I carefully set out fresh towels and a pristine white nightgown for the bride to wear. It must be pure white, unblemished by other colors. Not brown, not red, only white. This is one of the traditions for the wedding night. Why? Because it represents purity and cleanliness. In addition, it ensures that after intercourse if there is blood, it will be clearly visible. Red wouldn't show it as clearly. Only white. The wedding night outfit consists of four parts: The first garment is long, the second is about half-length, accompanied by a beautiful pair of underwear, and there's also a robe. It's a very complete set. A white towel is essential, and the bed sheet for that night must also be white. It can have a touch of flowers or a hint of gold, but it must be white.

Typically, I complete my duties at the wedding and do not accompany the couple to their room. I do, however, go in beforehand to light candles and set the scene. I leave them with a few verses from the Quran, for example, "May God protect you from Satan." I gently remind the groom that tonight she is his guest, and it's perfectly fine if they choose to simply rest. I suggest he prepare a selection of fruits, nuts, drinks, and water in the fridge, as one would for honored guests. I tell the bride to enter wearing the beautiful outfit we prepared for you. I direct the couple to share a meal and start with gentle caresses. Go slowly, take your time. I prompt the groom to stroke his wife softly and speak sweet words to her. Treat her with kindness. Be sure your touch is comforting to her. She will stay with you. She won't run away. She will be with you only if she feels mentally ready. Don't pressure her. I know you are excited, that this is your special night, but remember, no one will knock on your door to ask if you've consummated the marriage yet or not. There was a time when people would wait outside the door, but those days are gone."

There are rare cases where families demand proof. I tell her that this towel is hers — "Don't give it to anyone, even if they ask. If you want extra security, show it to his mother, but to no one else." Although people are more progressive today, I advise her to put the towel in a bag and hide it where he won't see it — for added security against unforeseen troubles. These are my quirks or perhaps my eccentricities, but also lessons drawn from my life experiences. I know of several instances where the husband was a shameless scoundrel — I apologize for speaking so bluntly — who later claimed his bride wasn't a virgin and he abandoned her. I tell her, "Hide it. After you've shown it to his mother, hide it. Just like that! There are brazen people out there, and you are smart. Now you are empowered, never let yourself be the weak one."

I take pride in being well-received on the other side too, the men's side, despite the delicate nature of the topics I address. Their acceptance goes beyond mere tolerance; they actively seek my counsel on matters they would never discuss with their sisters. Among them are truly shy men who invite me into their homes and ask their wives to consult with me. A woman arrived and shared that her husband urged her, "Go, go, spend time with Hiba." I don't take money for this; financial gain isn't my objective. This is my contribution, a labor of love from a place of deep concern. I once talked about this during a seminar-workshop with a group of Jews. No one understood my motives; they didn't grasp why I do this voluntarily. It just happens this way. But to me, volunteering offers a gentler, more graceful interaction. It is not an obligation, but rather something transcendent, a gift from the heart. I don't believe such support should be paid for.

When I finish volunteering, I return home to my husband, slipping into slumber as if the day had been like any other. There's no invoice, or bill to be settled, nothing to account for— that's it, my mission is complete. The most important thing is that the couple enjoys that first night. It matters deeply to me that the bride feels good. I don't care about anyone else. The night will pass, and whether or not they engage in intercourse, the most important thing is her well-being. That she has a beautiful day. Sometimes, I have no prior connection to the wedding in any way, not to the bride or the groom. Nothing. Yet, when I sense there might be an emergency, I feel compelled to go and be there.

Guiding brides and grooms is a wonderful vocation, but I am also approached with darker, more difficult matters, with secrets such as rape, and then I feel suffocated. The boundaries between my life and the secrets thrust upon me blur, and it's impossible to continue as usual, without thinking about their weight. [wipes away a tear]. Some secrets constrict my breathing. I'm not employed by the Department of Social Welfare, but people come to me for help, and I cannot refuse to listen. My role extends beyond being compassionate and loving, wanting everyone to feel good. I also serve as a guardian and protector, alert to danger and ready to sound a warning, if that is what's necessary. I strive to offer additional guidance so that people avoid missteps. Mistakes can occur, even instances where a wife's perceived consent might lead a couple to engage in acts that our tradition and culture deems forbidden in relationships between men and women. Awareness of this reality is what overwhelms me. I didn't think to talk about this, I didn't intend to share it. Let's change the subject. I don't feel good about discussing this element.

Realizing My Capabilities

The student advisor at the college, once asked me, "Who educated you? Who is your role model?" I replied that my education was a patchwork of influences. My parents educated me thirty percent, fifty percent I educated myself, and as to the remaining twenty percent, I am still a work in progress. I want to share the other things I do, beyond the academic sphere. I'll start with my home and myself within it. If I give myself the respect I deserve and listen to myself, that sets the foundation. I extend respect outward, listen, and educate myself, nurture my children, and ensure my husband receives the rights he deserves, without relinquishing my rights to him. Education begins at home. A person not only goes to school; they go out and conduct themselves well in the world; A smile to a passerby, a kind gesture — these too are contributions to society. I find myself mediating various disputes and navigating conflicts, almost as if I've set a personal goal to make a difference. I belong here, I am present, and I am committed to helping create a better living environment for us all. If I want my children to live in a better society, it is my responsibility to help build it.

Every Thursday, I bake batches of cookies, but I only sell a third. The rest I distribute to children and elderly who could use a little sweetness in their lives. My inspiration isn't just one person; it's everyone I meet. Yes, I am truly fulfilling myself. My husband trusts me completely. Even if I'm in the thick of things, he never calls to insist I rush home. He's a wonderful man. He supports me, gives me my space, helps with the children, listens to me, and respects my opinions. Yet, he doesn't crave excitement the way that I do. I'm like this; I have my own zest, I am fiery and full of energy, that's my own kind of spice. My husband, in contrast, possesses many skills, but acts quietly, with a more measured approach. His sense of calm frustrates me at times, but such is life. We complement each other perfectly. For instance, I don't speak English, and he does—he's an English teacher — so we complete each other in this way.

This is my home. I live here, and my children are here. I'm always cooking, always preparing something. It's as if I savor every moment. Of course, naturally, I'm happy — why wouldn't I be? Alhamdulillah (praise be to God), I am indeed happy. Why not? I'm always happy because I've chosen to be happy. I've learned to expect little from others, because by lowering my expectations, I avoid disappointment. A Bedouin woman faces many conflicts. We teach, learn, work, mother, cook, sell — we do it all, but often remain in the shadows. Now, I have a new dream, but I won't reveal it. I have many dreams, but lately, I've been cautious. Why? Because, unfortunately, there are those who steal dreams. I had dreams and plans spanning the next decade. Some will come to fruition, and some will not. I understand that life demands sacrifices. It's impossible to have it all; It's not possible to get everything. Even if you want both this and that, nothing can be perfect. You have to make sacrifices, and everything has its price. No matter how you look at it, compromise is always somewhat flawed.

Chapter IV
Bedouin Across the Negev:
Theoretical Perspectives on Social Issues

Introduction

Approximately 300,000 Bedouin are estimated to reside in the Negev. A significant portion live in Rahat and other state-established settlements, while about 29% inhabit "scattered" areas known as unrecognized villages. Mired in ongoing land disputes, these areas suffer from a lack of basic infrastructure such as water, electricity, and sewage systems. Since these villages are not recognized by State authorities, they lack local governance, as well as access to essential services, like healthcare and education (Kedar, Amara, & Yiftachel, 2017; 2018; Almasi, 2023).

The Bedouin community represents close to 2.7% of Israel's total population and about 15.6% of its Arab population, with 20.9% of Bedouin settlements ranked among the most socio-economically disadvantaged according to the Central Bureau of Statistics' socio-economic index. Bedouin society is characterized by its communal and patriarchal nature. Additionally, the unemployment rate in these communities is near 30%, and about half of the families live below the poverty line (Eyal and Tirosh, 2018; Alfasi-Henley, 2016). The seven permanent Bedouin towns are among the lowest in socio-economic standing in Israel, reflecting the severe socio-economic challenges faced by this community (Central Bureau of Statistics, 2023).

In 2007, the Authority for Development and Settlement of the Bedouin in the Negev was established, with its primary roles being the resolution of land ownership claims, the regularization of permanent residences, and the provision of infrastructure and public services in both existing and new settlements. Additionally, the Authority supports employment integration and coordinates educational, welfare, and community services (Abu-Rabia Queder, Morris, & Ryan, 2018; Yiftachel, Roded, & Kedar, 2016; Kark, 2024).

Bedouin customs are deeply rooted in tradition and conservative values, emphasizing strong family and tribal collectivism (Kark, 2023). Within these communities, the patriarchal family structure is evident in that women are largely dependent on the men in their families for support (Dwairy, 2004; Netzer 2015).

Bedouin society is characterized by its collectivism, where individuals identify themselves through their affiliation with the group, often the collective's well-being above personal interests (Finkelstein, 2010). Regarded as both a social and political entity, Bedouin tribes share not only customs and language but also a network of mutual commitments and robust familial bonds (Stewart, 2012; Yahal and Abu-Wajaj, 2021). The vast majority of Bedouins identify as devout Muslims, adhering to Islamic law (Sharia), which influences their daily practices—including prayer, fasting, and pilgrimage—through teachings derived from the Quran and the Sunnah (oral tradition), guiding their everyday activities in the spirit of Islam (Rubin, 2017).

The traditional, authentic leader among the Bedouins is the sheikh, whose role is passed down hereditarily and based on family affiliation. This position carries the authority and responsibility to govern the tribe, which includes signing the necessary approvals and documents that tribe members require for their own verification or authentication. Today, a new generation of leaders is emerging, seeking wider legitimacy to effectively represent the local population (Alsraiha, 2020).

The fertility rate within the Bedouin population is significantly higher than that of Arab families in Israel (Myers-JDC-Brookdale Institute, 2017). The practice of polygamy also contributes to the higher number of children in a single household. According to estimates by welfare authorities in the South, about 30% of Bedouin families in the region practice a polygamous lifestyle (Spector-Ben Ari, 2013b). Similar findings have been reported in other studies published over the last decade, which argue that not only is there no decline in the rate of polygamy, but rather that the phenomenon is also prevalent among the educated and the young (Elkrinawi & Slonim-Nevo, 2005; Spector-Ben Ari, 2013a). Although criminal law does not permit marriage to multiple women, many Bedouin men live with several women without being officially and legally married to them, thereby allowing polygamy to continue in practice (Spector-Ben Ari, 2013a). Some argue that the prevalence of polygamy in Bedouin society stems from Islamic beliefs, yet a closer examination of the Quran reveals only one verse that addresses polygamy: "If you can treat orphans justly, you may marry two, three, or four women. But if you cannot treat them justly, then only one."[15]

A rich body of literature delves into the lives of the Bedouins, exploring their culture, both their distant and recent history and their complex identity. Their ongoing struggle with the state over land registration rights remains a persistent issue on the public agenda. Amid the political chaos of the Israeli-Palestinian conflict, beliefs, stereotypes, primal fears, and positions have neither withstood the test of scrutiny nor fostered mutual understanding. The Israeli public sees the Bedouins, yet at the same time, they remain invisible within its collective perception.

In the stories of the seven women featured in this book, a tapestry of issues related to Bedouin society emerges, particularly through the experiences of its women: the struggles of young women to realize their right to education, family building, loss and mourning, growth from traumatic life crises, polygamy, concealment of harmful practices, ignorance in forming intimate

---

[15] *Quran,* Surat An-Nisa, verse 3. In the original:

وَإِنْ خِفْتُمْ أَلَّا تُقْسِطُواْ فِى ٱلْيَتَٰمَىٰ فَٱنكِحُواْ مَا طَابَ لَكُم مِّنَ ٱلنِّسَآءِ مَثْنَىٰ وَثُلَٰثَ وَرُبَٰعَ ۖ فَإِنْ خِفْتُمْ أَلَّا تَعْدِلُواْ فَوَٰحِدَةً أَوْ مَا مَلَكَتْ أَيْمَٰنُكُمْ ۚ ذَٰلِكَ أَدْنَىٰٓ أَلَّا تَعُولُواْ

relationships between men and women, and female leadership navigating between tradition and modernity. Hovering above all these are rigid patriarchal structures of unquestioned male dominance, it is notably religion which is perceived as a comforting, comprehensive support, offering encouragement and hope.

In this final chapter of the book, I will delve deeper into the topics that the women felt compelled to share through their narratives. As with any ethnographic inquiry, the broader picture remains somewhat imagined. The women recounting their tales aim to present a personal and intimate world, yet simultaneously, the researcher is able to discern elements common, in one way or another, to so many Bedouin women.

The Struggle for the Education of Bedouin Women

Higher Education as a Promised Land

Three centuries after the flourishing of the European Enlightenment, which championed freedom of thought, placed the individual at the center, advocated for equal educational rights, and favored academic knowledge over national, religious, and ethnic origins, young Bedouin women grapple with a traditional culture that perceives a real threat from freedom, skepticism, and the autonomy of the thinking individual. "You have denied me education even though you promised me before God. God will repay you for this," Amal reproached her father-in-law. After the advent of Islam initially brought progressive and humanistic views that opposed the degradation of women and encouraged seeing them as equals to men in rights and responsibilities, thousands of young Bedouin women like Kawkab, Amal, Adel, and others, continue to fight for their right to learn. These three narrators represent themselves; their stories are personal and intimate. They do not stand on public platforms representing other women but live day by day, striving to realize their dreams of securing higher education in a world that places barriers before their heartfelt desires. In this chapter, the narrative extends beyond their individual stories to encompass young Bedouin women across the Negev, for whom education is a beacon of their tribe's campfire, guiding their steps forward.

Traditional societal expectations view women as primarily responsible for managing the home and not venturing into the public sphere. The ease with which fathers in the family decide to halt their daughters' education after elementary school or during high school years compels those who wish to continue studying to engage in a relentless struggle just for the right to learn. "My sisters, both of them, did not study beyond the eighth grade. In our family, it was believed that girls who go to high school might adopt bad cultural habits and not remain loyal to the family," recounted Kawkab. The phrase "an educated woman is a problematic woman" can also be heard from educated Bedouin men, even those in professional careers. The belief that education undermines a woman's role in the home and her willingness to be submissive to her husband and his desires, erasing her own, reflects a patriarchal perspective that sees a woman's education as irrelevant to her life and her familial role. Moreover, we must consider that traditional societies view an adolescent girl as a potential threat to the family's honor, especially if she engages in a romantic relationship without being married. Understanding this, it becomes clear why there is immense pressure on young women to marry early, thereby aligning themselves with a man under whose protection the family honor is no longer at risk of being compromised. (Agbaria, 2015).

Unlike elementary education, where the participation rate among Bedouins in the Negev is nearly one hundred percent (similar to the rates in Jewish and Arab education), the gap in secondary education between the Bedouins and other sectors continues to widen. The dropout rate among girls occurs mainly during the transition from middle to high school, particularly in ninth grade, affecting about one-fifth of Bedouin girls. In unrecognized villages, where there are no high schools, the dropout rate is even higher, though there is no documentation of this in the State's statistical records (Abu-Rabia-Queder, 2017). When Amal's mother sent her six-year-old daughter to school for the first time, she told her, "You won't be with the sheep; you'll do something good and important." In doing so, she was rebelling against the reality she knew well, a reality that places women in a subordinate position in a society and that distances them from education. Twelve years later, she will stand under the hot sun on a hill, an hour's walk from home, watching from afar as her daughter waits by the road for a ride to her matriculation exam at school.

Studies on patriarchal societies show that women's education and their subsequent integration into the labor market are decisive factors in changing social consciousness (Abu-Rabia Queder, 2017). The revolution in the status of Bedouin women may be tied to the recognition and internalization of the economic potential inherent in education (Abu-Rabia, 2014). The revelation that women who have completed their studies at teacher training colleges are a stable economic force within the family after joining the educational system is like a wheel that cannot be turned back (see also Abu-Rabia-Queder & Arar, 2011). The connection between education and employment among Palestinians in Israel is not direct due to ethnic origins and the limitations imposed on their employment advancement in Israeli society. Nevertheless, within the Arab community in Israel, every employment category is based on achievements and personal skills (Abu-Rabia-Queder, 2017). Education creates hope for change, for new growth, and for the power to build a better world. "If you don't go study, your place will be in the pasture. You will be with the sheep all your life," said Amal's mother to her young daughter, and Kawkab, the fair-faced girl urged her father, who since her birth had seen her as a rising star amidst the bustling chaos of the family tent teeming with children, that he would never curtail her studies.

Kasr al-Sir is a small Bedouin village located west of Dimona, home to fewer than two thousand residents from the Hawashlah clan. In terms of culture, tradition, and socio-economic status, the villagers resemble other members of their tribe residing in nearby villages or scattered across the Negev. However, a conversation with a Bedouin researcher familiar with the Bedouin of the Negev reveals that a significantly higher percentage of girls from this village pursue higher education compared to those from other villages.[16] An attempt to understand this phenomenon suggested that the reason for the substantially larger number of girls pursuing further education might be due to the village's proximity to the Dimona-Be'er Sheva Road. This hypothesis was supported by past data linking the lack of public transportation from unrecognized Bedouin villages to the exclusion of women from the public workforce (Abu-Rabia-Queder, 2017). The bus station at the entrance to the village enables young women to travel to and from colleges and universities in an organized manner, without confronting accepted cultural norms that demand close supervision. "It's acceptable to travel on the bus," the men in the village would say, and the young women's morning departures for their studies is seen as an act that do not compromise their modesty, provided they return home before dark.

The issue of accessibility to education primarily traverses through space, starting with the physical distance from home to school, and then to college or university. The story of Amal's struggle for education is interwoven with obstacles along the way: initially, the journey to her elementary school, located four kilometers from their home, which she and her brother alternately traveled on foot and by donkey. The large wadi, whose winter water flow often blocked their path, surfaced repeatedly as an obstacle in her story. Later on, descriptions were added of her daily trek across open fields to the road where transportation to high school was available. All these journeys were all embarked upon under the scorching sun of summer or in a race against the fading light in the short days of winter, when darkness fell early, without regard for the end time of her matriculation exams. The extended darkness not only threatened Amal's personal safety but also put her father's approval of her continued education to the test. Kawkab also describes the challenges

---

[16] A Conversation with Qasem al-Zaraei'a, May 2018.

of physically getting to school: "I would walk for forty-five minutes each way. I don't even know the distance in kilometers, because we would take shortcuts through the hills instead of walking along the dirt road, which took longer. In the winter, sometimes I would get a lift that would bring me to school, but there wasn't always a vehicle available. Sometimes I would end up walking and getting soaked in the rain. Despite everything, I never missed a day of school."

The success of young Bedouin women in acquiring an education is tied not only to their studies themselves but also to their ability and determination to overcome accessibility challenges on their educational journey. Sarab Abu-Rabia-Queder (2017) notes that the lack of public transportation can reinforce patriarchal norms, such as the requirement for a man to accompany a woman when she leaves the village and restrictions on her hours of departure. Additionally, the absence of a basic education reduces the likelihood that women will obtain a driver's license and lead a more independent lifestyle. To navigate these difficulties, Bedouin women must constantly negotiate with the male figures in their families. In other words, — they are required to dismantle the alliances of oppression that restrict them. (Barakat, 2018).

Researchers examining behaviors that challenge submission to patriarchy among Muslim women in the Middle East (see, for example: Abu-Lughod, 2013; Mahmood, 2005) argue that any analysis of the actions of these pioneering women must be considered within a social, religious, and historical context, and cannot be simply interpreted in terms of oppression, but rather in the unique way these women perceive their own actions. Kawkab, who observed her father ending her sisters' education at a young age, began negotiating with him when she was still a little girl, understanding even then that education was not a privilege automatically granted to daughters: "Ever since I was young, whenever my father told me he loved me, I would immediately say to him, 'Just don't stop my education.' It was like a game between us, but I knew it would firmly imprint in my father's mind—that Kawkab would go to school and not give up." Some young women relied on their older brothers, especially those who had attained higher education, whose authority often countered their father's demands for the daughters to remain at home. Amal had to wait seven years until her brother returned from studying medicine abroad to support her further education. Faiza learned Hebrew at the non-profit organization "Step Forward" after becoming widowed, and without her family's knowledge. Her brothers supported her driving lessons while her father opposed them. In contrast, Hiba capitalized on the window of opportunity to secretly take driving lessons, while her brother, a lawyer interning an hour away from home, was absent. Kawkab was confined at home to prevent her from attending the final exam of her master's studies, and when she finally appeared at the college, the tremendous struggle she had endured to get there was evident. Each of these women has a story of ongoing negotiation, whether direct or indirect, that they conducted with the male figures — the unquestioned authorities in family decision-making.

Only two of the women did not report a struggle to gain their family's approval for their studies: Adel, whose father is a university lecturer; and Hanan, whose mother was born in central Israel and whose father lived in the central region for many years. It seems that the parents' education or simply residing for many years in a mixed city contributes to the perception that women's education enhances their chances of attaining higher education and succeeding in the job market thereafter, without compromising the family's honor (Ben-Asher, Sabar-Ben Yehoshua, & Albador, 2020).

To effect change, a change agent is required — an individual or entity responsible for creating the shift, and in this case, it's the persistence of Bedouin women in pursuing higher education. Who are these agents of change? Research literature often claims that mothers enforce traditional demands and restrict their daughters' life realm. For this reason, they are referred to in the literature as "jailers of patriarchy" (Hochschild, 2003). In traditional societies, mothers tend to subjugate their daughters to societal structures by enforcing social dictates, as part of the social construction they experienced in their childhood and adolescence (Ghanim, 2009). However, while the stories of the women in this book reveal that the support of a father or an older brother is crucial, some mothers also played a pivotal role, as was evident, for example, in Amal's story. Barakat (2018), who studied the struggle of women for education in the Druze society, found that when young women are able to enlist their mothers in their efforts to obtain higher education, the likelihood of successfully realizing this aspiration significantly increases.

When analyzing the struggle for education among Bedouin women, one cannot overlook the economic conditions of this population. Poverty and low economic capability act as barriers to receiving an academic education, and the link between poverty and education is one of the leading indicators in economics (see for example Almagor-Lotan, Bar, and Levi, 2010). The Bedouin community is among the poorest in Israel (Abu-Bader & Gottlieb, 2013), but in this traditional community, discussing poverty is considered shameful (Rodnitzky and Abu-Ras, Gribiea, Ben-Asher, & Kupferberg, 2019). The financial challenges of pursuing academic studies are not presented in the narratives of these women as a standalone issue, but rather as anecdotes that illustrate the complex conversations that they had to engage in with the men in their families about the right to allocate financial resources for education, along with both the strength and effort required from them to meet the financial burden of their studies.

In most developed countries, poverty is defined in economic terms as relative. A person is considered poor if their standard of living is significantly below the average within their society. However, newer approaches describe "narrative poverty," based on the individual's feelings (Liblich, 2017; Shidlowsky, 2018). In her words – Amal described bonding with another student as impoverished as herself. They would sit together in a secluded room at the college, eating pita bread because they couldn't afford to buy food from the cafeteria. Her story highlights the shame that often accompanies poverty: "We didn't let anyone see what we were eating. The other girls studying with me would all go to buy food at the cafeteria. They all dressed nicely and would order a wide variety of food dishes. We had nothing. We felt ashamed that we didn't have money." Other descriptions illustrate poverty in the context of financial demands related to fulfilling mandatory academic tasks: "On practical fieldwork days, we were required to prepare crafts and activities for the kindergarten where we were interning. At the end of the day, after all the girls in the class had finished their assignments in the workshop, we used to take the leftovers from the trash and create beautiful projects. When they saw our works, they would say, 'Wow, what wonderful work you've done.' And yes: 'When I arrived at college, one of the students approached me asking for money to buy a farewell gift for the kindergarten teacher and the students. I took out the twenty shekels I had and was left with nothing until the end of the month.'"

Although physical and economic accessibility to higher education and cultural constraints are significant barriers for Bedouin women pursuing advanced studies, the greatest contributing factors to the success of their struggle are personal motivation and internal drive. It appears that these are the strongest and most crucial force propelling these women, as described in studies focusing on the motivation of Arab young women in education (e.g., Gribiea et al., 2019). Self-determination theory identifies three basic psychological needs: belonging, competence, and autonomy. Fulfilling these needs contributes to optimal development, intrinsic motivation, commitment, and the individual's social adaptation (Deci & Ryan, 2012; Ryan & Deci, 2000). Research conducted among Bedouin female students at a college by Adnan Gribiea and others (2019) found that these Bedouin women do not succumb to the various challenges they face; rather, they confront these obstacles with determination. Time and time again, women emphasized the need to excel in their studies despite the significant difficulties they face and despite the obstacles that sometimes seem insurmountable.

Contemplating the stories of Amal and Kawkab allows us to discern in their narratives what Spector-Mersel (2011) refers to as the "bottom line" or the endpoint: when these women summarize the central axis of their lives that defines their value and success, they focus on their power to achieve their goal — securing higher education despite all obstacles and constraints. The overarching narrative, or "big story," of Arab and Bedouin women is interwoven with numerous "short stories," linked by a strong passion for learning and advancement. In the eyes of these women, education is not merely about obtaining a certificate of knowledge or completing courses containing certain content, but primarily a method to accumulate cultural and social capital, enabling them to present themselves as educated within their communities and to construct their lives with greater control and a relative reduction of the segregating and discriminatory restrictions characteristic of traditional Bedouin society (Abu-Rabia-Queder & Karplus, 2013; Arar & Shapira, 2016). However, their exposure to education, which also influences their perceptions, confronts them with fundamental issues related to their personal, professional, and national identities, perceptions of family, challenges of married life, as well as, issues related to choosing a spouse and building a family (Abu-Rabia-Queder & Weiner-Levy, 2013; Ben-Asher et al., in press).

The issue of education for the Bedouins in general, and Bedouin women in particular, is currently on Israel's national agenda. Accessibility of higher education for the Arab community has been defined as one of the main issues in the multi-year plan of the higher education system (Council for Higher Education, 2017). However, implementation at the national level is only partial. There is hardly any focus on public awareness or dissemination of information within the Bedouin community to promote women's education and to change traditional social perceptions that hinder women from advancing to higher education. It appears that public policy, which promotes education by changing community perceptions while respecting Bedouin tradition and culture, could be as effective — if not more so — than budgets allocated to bodies and organizations for developing academic and vocational education programs, which are often inaccessible to many young women. If one wished to learn about ways to assist young Bedouin women, it would be wise to sit down with Kawkab, Amal, Adel, and other educated young women to deeply understand the challenges they face. They know every stone in the road, including the stumbling blocks, the flash floods, the scorching sun on their way to school, and the darkness that does not wait for their return at the end of the school day. They are familiar with the disdainful looks from men and the prevalent statements among some women that pursuing education is linked to the violation of their honor and the modesty expected of them. They know the necessity of mastering Hebrew and English immediately upon finishing high school, where only a limited amount of time is allocated to these subjects. They are also well aware of the intense pressure directed at them to marry as early as possible and to start families.

It is possible that if higher education in the Bedouin community is not only defined as a national social goal, but also implemented as such, Bedouin girls would receive scholarships enabling a dignified existence during their studies, and the path to higher education would be paved for more and more young women. The wall of resistance cannot be built on the economic burden associated with acquiring higher education. The challenge of pursuing higher education is not exclusive to Bedouin women in the Negev, but crosses borders and is common to Arab women in general (Yeganeh, 2012). Their strength lies in the joining of many young women to this headstrong and determined group. Social changes require vision, setting goals, pooling resources, and a foundation of values for a more just society.

In the long and heavy hijabs, which cover their bodies even on sweltering days and are meant to shield them from forbidden gazes, these women navigate daily between worlds, understanding that they are the true bridge between them. They are the keystones of the gates of education, through which, in a few years, today's girls will pass. The stories of Kawkab, Amal, and Adel presented in this chapter are a tribute to the thousands of young women who, at this very moment, are carrying the torch of a revolution that can no longer be stopped.

Adonis's poem about his father and his relationship to the spiritual world acquired through education is a rare lyrical expression of the aspirations held by young Bedouin women for higher education:

> My father was a farmer,
> He loved and wrote poetry.
> He did not read
> If the poem did not place a loaf of bread upon his head.
> (Adonis, 2013, p. 130)

Bedouin Students in Jewish Schools

The Israeli education system is segregated into Jewish and Arab schools, including Bedouin schools. Over the years, the separation between the sectors has been largely accepted by both communities: The Jewish society has supported it mainly due to fears of close relationships between Jewish and Arab students, which could complicate the emphasis on Jewish and national themes in the curriculum. The Arab society has favored separate schools because the Arab educational system is perceived as contributing to the preservation of the Palestinian national identity emerging among Israeli Arabs. Exceptions are schools that champion joint education for Jews and Arabs, such as the Weizmann School in Jaffa (see Levi and Shavit, 2015) and the school in Neve Shalom.

In recent years, a noticeable change has emerged at the grassroots level, not as part of the formal policy of the Ministry of Education. Studies indicate an increase in the number of Arab students attending the Jewish education system. Although there are concerns in the Arab community about the potential impact on the children's identity, parents compromise for the sake of better and more affluent schooling (Kadari-Ovadia and Kashti, 2018). In some cases, beyond seeking high academic achievement, students and their parents aspire to integrate into "Israeli-ness." For this purpose, they are willing to adopt Hebrew as the language of instruction for core subjects and to study additional subjects including the Bible, Israeli heritage, and civics, thereby exposing themselves to Zionist-Israeli education. It appears that these early signs of integration in the Israeli education system are not the result of a directed policy from the education authorities, but rather are expanding from the bottom up, driven by the parents themselves and from initiatives by civil society organizations. The reasons motivating Arab parents to send their children to Jewish schools vary: some believe that the quality of education in the Jewish schools is superior; others want their children to learn standard Hebrew to assist in integrating into the Israeli-Jewish society; some see Jewish-State education as a solution to their children's special needs; and others choose it as a refuge from hostility and vengeance (for example, among families where the father has assisted the State in security matters).

The trend of Arab students integrating into Jewish schools also exists among the Bedouins, albeit with a distinct character (Abd al-Karim, 2015; Shavit, Shweid, Dalasha, and Ofek, 2014). The Bedouin population, as a whole, was characterized by a high motivation for an early dropout of girls from schools. Data shows that the academic achievements of Bedouin students are significantly lower than those of students in the Arab and Jewish education systems across all age groups, and the percentage of Bedouin students eligible for a matriculation diploma is the lowest in the country (Weininger, 2013). Given the dire state of education in the Bedouin sector, some educated families prefer to send their children to Jewish schools in hopes of facilitating their future integration into higher education institutions. This choice is made through a comparison between the Bedouin and Jewish educational systems and parental awareness of the gap between them.

How does the educational environment impact the integrated minority group within it? Numerous researchers have explored how minority youth cope in majority-group schools (e.g., Marbley & Bonner, 2007; Ogbu & Simons, 1998). Their research highlight issues of adaptation and difficulties in social and cultural integration, as well as academic disparities between the groups. Ogbu (2004) identified significant differences between the behavior of students from voluntary minority groups and those from involuntary minority groups: the achievements of minorities who voluntarily study in majority-group schools were higher than those of involuntary minorities. He argued that the reason for this achievement gap is that students who choose to study in majority-group schools adopt the prevailing cultural models of the school, often at the expense of emphasizing their own cultural models.

Studies on the interaction between Arab Palestinian learners in Israel and Jewish learners within the educational environment have predominantly been conducted among university students, with only a few examining this interaction in high school settings (Hamesa, 2011). In two studies on Arab high school girls studying in Jewish schools (Ben-David, 2003; Ghanem, 2007), the young women reported that after completing their studies, they developed a unique identity different from that of other women in the Palestinian society, yet also distinct from the identity of Jewish women. They spoke of feeling like outliers, different and even estranged from both communities, as if they were in a separate space of belonging, or as expressed in their words, "neither inside nor outside." The drive for education was a primary motivation, but it was accompanied by experiences of marginalization and a sense of disconnection from their own culture, particularly in terms of their proficiency in Arabic.

Among the stories of the women featured in the book, Adel's account is particularly remarkable because her father had already broken through the barriers to education in the previous generation. As a child, his parents sent him to a school in the North to receive a high-quality education that would enable him to meet the admission requirements of academic institutions in Israel. In the 1940s, only the children of the sheikhs were educated in the school in Be'er Sheva. Even after the establishment of the State of Israel and the enactment of the Compulsory Education Law in 1949, there was no significant change for more than twenty years. The nomadic lifestyle of the Bedouins and their dispersion across the Negev in the early decades of the State made it difficult to establish an educational system for them. It was only in the 1970s, with the beginning of their urbanization process, that the implementation of the Compulsory Education Law began in their settlements, including the establishment of educational institutions in unrecognized villages and towns (Rodnitzky and Abu Ras, 2011).

Children of educated parents grow up in families that recognize the value of education. This advantage is reserved for a small elite group among the Bedouins of the Negev. However, Adel's story reveals that even this group of young men and women pays a heavy price. Adel's account is augmented by the stories of seven young Bedouin women from the Negev region, which were not included in the book. These young women, who studied in the same Jewish high school as Adel, all hold advanced academic degrees in selective and challenging fields such as: medicine, para-medical professions, business administration, and more, and are integrated into their respective professional careers (Ben-Asher et al., 2020). Their personal stories are not homogeneous, just as the other women's stories presented in the book vary significantly from one another. Each one possesses a unique and personal narrative identity. Yet, a common narrative emerges among them as Bedouin students in a Jewish school. An overarching message from all the interviews is that academic success often comes at a significant personal cost of sacrificing the ability to live a traditional-religious lifestyle — one that does not continuously negotiate the right to freedom. The interviewees characterize their education in a Jewish school as a transformative experience that molded them into strong women who steadfastly uphold their rights. However, this very strength often leads to conflicts with their surroundings as they strive to balance their assertiveness with the desire to remain integrated within their society.

For Adel's parents, education is a supreme value, and it stands at the top of their priorities. Adel made every effort to excel as a student in the Jewish school, despite facing challenges throughout the years:

To this day, I am deeply grateful to my parents for affording me the opportunity to study in those schools. A large part of my identity and who I am today is tied to those schools, but also to the fact that I might always sit on the fence, never truly belonging to any side. Only those who have sat on the fence know how much pain accumulates in the body from sitting there.

It was only after completing her studies that Adel confronted questions of identity. At a forum on "Pluralism in Education" in which she participated, Adel shared:

I felt like I didn't belong in either place, especially after I finished twelfth grade and started working with the Arab and Bedouin populations. I began to feel this deficiency in literary Arabic. For me, Hebrew is my mother tongue. Everything else I received from home — the values, the religious commandments, its values, its culture.

The relationships of Bedouin students, particularly the female students, who are educated in Jewish schools, are circumscribed by red lines. Naturally, the expanding social connections of these adolescents include experiences of first love with the opposite sex. In a Western liberal society, the space for exploring relationships between genders is much broader than in traditional and insular societies, where a strict separation of genders is maintained. Bedouin female students come from a society where honor and modesty are the most valued aspects in the upbringing of a girl.

How did the Bedouin girls who studied at the Jewish school cope with the "red lines" clearly drawn for them in Bedouin society? "I come from a Bedouin environment where there are all these prohibitions for girls. Jewish girls don't have these restrictions," said one of Adel's young Bedouin friends who was interviewed for the research (Ben-Asher et al., in press). She continued, describing how she asked her father to allow her to attend her classmates' birthday parties, but he refused, fearing that these parties would involve close interactions between boys and girls. "That was a red line for him," the young woman said, adding that in retrospect, she is grateful to him for shielding her from what she now perceives as a danger. At the same time, she acknowledged the difficulty she faced dealing with these prohibitions: "It's hard to feel like I'm just here for the studies and don't really have friends to spend time with."

The girls' response to what was marked as a "red line" was to isolate themselves by keeping a distance from the rest of the students. Part of enforcing this caution against forming close relationships between the Bedouin girls and the Jewish boys was imposed on the group of Bedouin boys and girls themselves, as a sort of "social guard": "In my class, there were also Bedouin boys. They were my friends, but not in the same way as the Jewish boys, because there was some kind of barrier, there were boundaries," one of the girls explained. Her friend added: "We Arabs would sit together at the back of the class. It was our choice."

While the social segregation between Jewish and Bedouin students is distinct and noticeable, the gap between the Bedouin girls attending Jewish schools and their Bedouin peers persists in practice, even if it isn't overtly acknowledged in social contexts. Adel shared that she barely had connections with her extended family:

I always felt like a 'strange bird' there. At family events, I felt that everyone was scrutinizing me, and only later did I understand that these looks were because my mother was 'Northern' — different in appearance, culture, and mentality, and I, like her, looked different.

Other Bedouin girls experienced the cultural transition daily:

In the morning, I am there, in a beautiful and pastoral place, learning, and they invest in me and give me all the understanding in the world. Then I come home to a place with a different language and behavior. It's always either this way or that way. You can't be both.

Adel chose to follow her mother's path and dress in attire accepted in Western society. The clear messages from her Bedouin family influenced her to dress modestly, yet in a way that did not set her apart from the Jewish students who studied with her and came from traditional families. For Adel, the question of dress was seemingly resolved thanks to her mother, who had already led the change. For the other young Bedouin women studying alongside her, clothing was deeply intertwined with significant explorations of identity:

On the kibbutz, we would wake up and wear whatever we wanted, just going with the flow. You have the freedom to do what is good for you and what you want. When you return home and go out to your uncles, you need to put on a shirt that is a bit longer. The entire process of adapting and integrating into society often begins with something as basic as choosing which shirt to wear.

Maintaining their traditional attire was seen by them as a way of preserving their identity: "We kept to our traditions. We didn't show up in bodysuits and short pants," one of them said. The interviewees made a variety of clothing decisions, and it seemed that behind the question of what to wear was a deeper issue of identity and the liminal feeling of being "neither here nor there." "I'm a bit of everything," one young woman said to summarize the matter.

Like Adel's story, for the other young Bedouin women who studied with her, once their parents decided to enroll them in the

Jewish high school, they were tasked with a single mission: to successfully complete their education in a position primed for entry into prestigious academic tracks (Ben-Asher et al., in press). With their studies completed, the path to these higher studies was paved for them. While their peers in the Bedouin community were preoccupied with engagements and weddings, these young women found themselves confronting a socio-cultural divide: military service, (the natural continuation for graduates of Jewish schools), was not an option for them, and early marriage did not align with the expectation that they would enter academia. Marriages in the Bedouin society are rooted in social arrangements and are conducted to maintain the familial-tribal structure. Thus, a spouse is chosen by the family as part of a social transaction, a notion radically different from the liberal Western ideal of free choice in personal relationships. For the Bedouin women educated in Jewish schools, viewing marriage as a transaction represents a denial of their self-conception as individuals who autonomously and independently decide their own lives. It is important to remember that the age for marriage in Bedouin society ranges from seventeen to twenty-two. Beyond this age, the chances of the girls marrying significantly decrease.

Graduates of the Jewish school reported difficulty in finding a Bedouin partner who shares the liberal views on women and gender equality that they were taught at school. The young women described a reality where differing worldviews and mentalities pose significant barriers to forming romantic relationships and getting married. One graduate shared:

I don't want to marry just any Bedouin. I've reached a point in my life where I am truly independent. I really don't feel like I need a man. I know that the message in

Arab society for a woman is: 'You need to get married.' It's seen as a mandatory life goal for us, the ultimate destination for a woman. That's not my sole objective, it's just a part of my life. I'm independent and not prepared to be a wife just to sit at home and cook for him.

Her friend said, "You go to the university, you study with friends, and you're having fun, and you really feel like a young woman. Then you start working, you have a salary. So, you're having fun, and you buy whatever you want. That's what interested me. I wasn't interested in going off to have babies and get married," and she added, "A lot of guys passed through my parent's home trying to start a relationship with me, and I rejected them. My parents asked, 'Why do you reject him? Stop already. What's so bad about him?' The last time I rejected a potential suitor, my brother asked me, 'Do you want to marry someone Jewish?'"

The young, educated women, graduates of the Jewish high school, are intimately familiar with the mismatch between what they perceive as a good, harmonious partnership and the reality they must confront: "I love the progress I've made in my career. I feel that I have room to grow, I have my autonomy. I can do things on my own, without the approval of either men, or society," she quickly adds, with a sense of sadness and a recognition of reality, "Perhaps that's why I'm still not married." Moreover, those educated Bedouin women who are married still experience a gap in viewpoints between themselves and their husbands: "My husband quickly realized that we have completely different opinions about women in the Bedouin sector, about higher education, and about a variety of other issues. I think that's precisely what he was looking for — something a bit different. On the flip side, [she laughs] "sometimes he feels it's too much."

The success of all the Bedouin girls in completing the Jewish high school and integrating into higher academic studies signifies a victory in the path their parents had envisioned for them, namely, to break through the barriers of the failing Bedouin educational system and reach a stage where they could compete for prestigious academic tracks. To achieve this, parents were prepared to face internal family opposition and bear a financial burden over the years. The young Bedouin women adopted these expectations, and their shared narrative highlights their success in meeting the challenge placed before them. They proudly recounted their struggles with pride while supporting and emphasizing their stories of success. Failures, anxieties, and the costs paid by the interviewees as former students and as young women at present were almost inadvertently mentioned in their stories, hinted at only superficially in a way that allows understanding only by reading between the lines. In their accounts, one can indirectly hear defiance against a society entrenched in traditional patterns, echoing conflicts against the backdrop of their desire to choose their partners and build marital lives that reflect the personal perceptions they have shaped. Education, freedom, gender equality, and the right to autonomously manage their lives are not represented in the traditional identity of the Bedouin society, and often directly contradict its established norms. Parental support, which shielded them from social pressures during their studies, is no longer sufficient. The question of identity, which was suppressed during their youth, reemerges as a central issue requiring personal definition:

> I am Arab first, then, Muslim, Bedouin, and Israeli. That is my identity. There is no escaping it, and I am actually proud of it. But there is a difference between how I define my identity and where I think I belong. I don't feel a sense of belonging anywhere. (Ben-Asher et al., 2020)

The stories of Adel and other young Bedouin women who attended Jewish schools (see also Albadur, 2018 on young Bedouin women;

Barakat, 2018 on young Druze women; Hamesa, 2011 on young Arab women) raise two significant ethical and educational questions. The first concerns how Bedouin children grapple with constructing their identities during adolescence within a peer group that is not their own; the second involves the emotional support and psychological assistance required to cope with the tensions and conflicts posed by their pluralistic circumstances. These two areas — identity and emotion — are interconnected and influence their future choices in academic paths, society, employment, and relationship-building. Adel, who experienced a family crisis, expressed a strong need to prove to herself that she could manage alone without her husband and raise her children by herself. She summed this up in one sentence, "I can reach the summit, whatever the cost may be."

The establishment of a family is largely dependent on how Bedouin adolescents, who study in Jewish schools, resolve their identity crisis. Adel and her schoolmates are on a journey that began with their education in a Jewish school and continues with the complex portrait presented in this chapter.

As I close this chapter, part of a poem by Rachel Shapira resonates within me: I set off walking on my path. / The one who loved me will return to your fields — / From the desert. / And he will understand — I lived among you / like a wildflower." ("Like a Wildflower," Shapira, 1972). It is likely that other poems will resonate in these women's hearts, and that they are unfamiliar with this one, but the bitter taste of alienation and solitude was an inseparable part of their lives.

Bedouin IDF Widows

Death is Predetermined

Bereavement in the Bedouin society possesses unique characteristics from religious, cultural, and social perspectives. Islam views death —as it does birth — as the will of God. Bedouins believe that from the day they are born, their day of death is inscribed upon their foreheads, and they cannot dispute their "inscribed" destiny. A Bedouin proverb states: "Death is predetermined," meaning, death is a privilege, and a funeral is seen as the beginning of the journey back to God. One of the well-known Hadiths[17] about the Prophet Muhammad, recorded in the collection of Sahih al-Bukhari, addresses the believer's obligation to accept the decree of death graciously and without complaint. Expressions of difficult emotions such as anger and disappointment are seen as a lack of harmony with God's will (Rubin and Yassin-Ismail, 2006). The Arab writer Ayman Sikseck also depicted the Muslim attitude towards the deceased in his novel *"Tishreen"* (2016):

> You know, in Islam it is said that immediately after a person is buried and we turn our backs on the grave for the first time to leave the cemetery, it is a commandment to forget the deceased. It is a commandment to stop crying. For until we forget the deceased, we do not allow them to rest or meet the Creator. (p. 205)

In Bedouin society, mourning processes are founded on the belief that the grave of the deceased is not a place for visits or memorial

---

17 The Hadith (الحـديـث) is a collection of stories and sayings passed down orally from generation to generation about the life of the Prophet Muhammad. This collection holds a canonical status for Muslims and is considered the second most important text after the Quran.

ceremonies. The grave itself is simple — a stone bearing the name of the departed and the date of burial. The societal representation of remembrance is non-memory. It is permissible to keep photographs and personal items, but there is no tradition of visitation to the grave or commemoration. The Muslim religion allocates three days of mourning, after which family members are expected to begin organizing their lives anew. For Bedouin IDF widows, this reorganization encompasses both partners in the journey of bereavement: the husband's family and the Ministry of Defense, which accompanies her through the rehabilitation process (Ben Asher and Bukak-Cohen, 2017).

Enlistment in the Army in Bedouin Society: "Cause for Excommunication" or Source of Pride?

Nearly two hundred Bedouin soldiers have fallen since the founding of the State during their military service or under circumstances related to combat. Although the Ministry of Defense does not disclose precise figures out of respect for individual privacy, the number of Bedouin IDF widows is estimated to be in the several dozens. Any discussion concerning these widows necessitates an understanding of the Bedouin society's stance on military enlistment itself.

While in the Jewish population, military service is part of the hegemonic culture and national values, and bereaved families are perceived as a societal nobility that represents and reflects the values of sacrifice and mobilization of the society (Ben-Asher & Lebel, 2010; Lebel, 2011), in Bedouin society, especially since the first Intifada in the mid-1980s, military enlistment is considered contrary to the core social values, and sometimes even to religious values (although, in truth, the religion does not prohibit it). In the words of Faiza, the complex relationship with the military emerged between the lines. It is evident that beneath the surface, openly or secretly, some political beliefs and opinions see military enlistment as a detriment to the Palestinian national struggle.

> I can't recall exactly when he started talking about enlisting in the Army. I told him that joining the Israeli Army was "haram." Israeli soldiers are fighting Palestinians near Hebron, Nablus, and Ramallah, so if something bad happened to them, God would not help us. My father said that Bedouins shouldn't join the Army and that it's shameful to enlist in the IDF. Ironically, in Ali's family, they said that the Army belongs to our State, and it's an honor to be a soldier.

Faiza and Sana, whose stories are featured in the second chapter of the book, are two of the seven widows I met during a study focused on culturally-sensitive mourning, specifically on how IDF widows cope with bereavement (Ben-Asher and Bokek-Cohen, 2017). This research found that all the widows perceived mourning as a private experience. The processes of commemoration, which conveys the significance of the fallen soldier's sacrifice to the public sphere, do not occur in Bedouin society: not one of them described visits to the cemetery, or Memorial Day for fallen IDF soldiers. The ceremonies held at military cemeteries are not part of Bedouin culture and tradition. In this context, it should be noted that while a monument for the Bedouin soldier has been established in the northern part of the country, its remote location and lack of connection to Bedouin tradition have resulted in the site holding little significance for most of the widows.

When examining the commemoration methods assisted by the Ministry of Defense, it becomes clear that most are not suitable for the families of Bedouin fallen soldiers. Commemorative corners, the inauguration of a Torah scroll, the establishment of memorial sites, public activities like remembrance evenings and sports events, volunteering in IDF camps, scholarship grants, and the naming of public buildings after the fallen (Drori-Gohar, 2011) – none of these align with the culture and traditions of Islam. The issue is not one of deliberate exclusion, but rather a disconnect between the nature of commemoration and the essence of Bedouin culture. None of the widows' stories shared in this book, nor in the five additional accounts documented, include instances of mistreatment stemming from their husbands' deaths in the military. However, it is evident that while the State recognizes these women's loss, this acknowledgment is not valued within Bedouin society.

From the stories of Faiza and Sana, there are no collective national themes linked to the valor of their deceased husbands or the circumstances surrounding their deaths. Instead, intimate snapshots of life arise, each folds within it an entire world: the baby Ilham, wrapped in the chick-patterned blanket her father bought — her father, whom she will never meet; the moment the bitter news was delivered, just as the bread for the party celebrating her daughter's birth was nearly done baking, and Faiza's frantic dash home with the baby in her arms, to a house already filled with notifiers and comforters; the night Sana fell asleep waiting for a call from Ibrahim and the morning she awoke to a changed world; the funeral she herself was not permitted to attend. These personal moments cause the heartstrings to tremble, years after that dreadful day. Yet they are always depicted as private experiences, devoid of societal and national representation, in contrast to, for example, the descriptions of Jewish IDF widows (Ben-Asher & Bokek-Cohen, 2019). Unlike military bereavement, which is recognized and socially esteemed in Israel, Bedouin IDF widows grapple with neglected grief: their loss is not honored, and at times is even marked by inferiority due to the lack of public-social appreciation and national significance.

In the narratives of Faiza, Sana, and other women from the study on Bedouin IDF widows (Ben Asher and Bokek-Cohen, 2019), a profound chasm divides their lives before and after the tragedy. Each woman carries her own personal narrative along the long, arduous path to recovery. Common to all is their social status as Bedouin IDF widows. Within the internal social hierarchy of Arab society, the social status of a widow is considered lower than that of a married woman, and upon her husband's death, she is expected to exhibit a vulnerability that signifies her dependency on family and men. However, a widow's status is slightly better than that of a divorced woman (Meler, 2014). According to traditional views, the community sees the widows and their children as part of the deceased husband's extended household. The family is expected to provide for their livelihood, and the children's education, and oversee the widow. With the husband's death, the role of maintaining the code related to honor and shame associated with the widow shifts to the men in the family. Thus, widows remain subject to strict social supervision that greatly limits their independence and their ability to venture beyond the immediate vicinity of their home, often losing the relative independence they had while married. If a widow refuses this arrangement, she may be forced to separate from her children and leave them to live with their father's family.

The status of Bedouin IDF widows is exceptional compared to other Bedouin widows: while all widows are generally required to rely on familial support, primarily for financial reasons, IDF widows receive a pension from the Ministry of Defense, thereby lessening their dependence on the extended family. This ability to sustain themselves and their children economically challenges, at least financially, the social norm of male supervision over them. The demand by Sana's brother-in-law to transfer her compensation payments to him is not an isolated incident. Many widows face similar financial demands and are often compelled to assert themselves against such pressures, sometimes with the support of Ministry of Defense representatives.

The crossing of boundaries by these women from the confined family space to the public sphere is palpably manifested not only in managing the family's finances and making decisions about the education and schooling of their children but also in a variety of other interactions, such as learning to drive, purchasing a vehicle, and pursuing further education. Faiza's insistence on getting a driver's license, and her father's opposition to it, were not coincidental. The acquisition of a license and subsequently the ability to travel from home to shopping centers, or the city, challenge the traditional code that generally subjugates women and specifically widows. The mobility of a woman signifies a move beyond the family's closely monitored territory into the public domain. This is not just a physical departure, but it also carries symbolic, social, and cultural significance. Unlike Sana, who learned to drive during high school with her mother's encouragement and even bought a car when she got married, for Faiza, as for other women interviewed for the study, the driving license and the car they purchased (or "the vehicle," as they referred to it) symbolized their struggle for independence.

Depiction of the mourning process in the stories of the widows aligns with the loss processes described in the literature on bereavement (Rubin, Malkinson, and Witztum, 2016; Silverman & Nickman, 1996; Witztum, 2000). The widows spoke of the shock associated with receiving the bitter news, the difficulty of accepting the loss as reality, and subsequently, feelings of helplessness, anger, guilt, and deterministic thinking about fate. In their life stories, it was also possible to discern a sense of acceptance and adaptation to the altered reality (Ben-Asher and Bokek-Cohen, 2017, 2019).

It appears that the journey of coping with bereavement for Bedouin IDF widows is more complex and convoluted than the loss process described in the bereavement literature. Forming a new partnership and remarrying are possible almost exclusively within the deceased husband's family, and in any case, these would be polygamous marriages. For four months and ten days following their husband's death, the widows are forbidden from remarrying. This restriction ensures that the widow is not pregnant with the child of the deceased. After this period, Bedouin women face pressure to remarry. For Bedouin IDF widows, the motivation to remarry is not financial support, but rather a matter of social status to maintain the widow's honor within the family. Faiza chose not to remarry, partly because she was unwilling to be the second wife in a polygamous family. Despite living independently with her children and not moving to live with her father, he still oversaw her, setting limitations on her movements and lifestyle. Sana married Ibrahim's brother, hoping he would assist with raising the children. Her main disappointment came after she agreed to have a child together. Sana shared that she feels independent, and after improving her Hebrew and education, she is more aware of her capabilities and does not need a man for her day-to-day life. Ironically, her close relationship with Ibrahim's first wife provides her support, and the two women, having learned to coexist in a shared household, continue their lives together even after becoming widows.

The question of how willing members of a minority group, especially women, are to accept assistance from external entities, particularly when the help comes from care providers of the majority group, receives a complex response. Palestinians seeking help from Israel are undermining two fundamental principles: The first is that "one does not air one's dirty laundry in public," meaning personal and family issues are not to be exposed to outside institutions; the second principle is "Maktub," — meaning, the faith in fate. Generally, Palestinian women who dare to seek external support often face stringent scrutiny (Popper-

Giveon & Al-Krenawi, 2010; Savaya, 1998), given that service providers, like social workers, are perceived as representatives of a colonial government that oppresses Palestinians and exploits community vulnerabilities to cause further harm (Meler, 2015).

The social identity of the widows encompasses four components: Palestinian, Bedouin, women, and widows. Almost all the widows recounted how the Defense Ministry does not assist, yet in the same breath, they described how they relied on the social workers of the Defense Ministry's Rehabilitation Division. To an outside observer, this inconsistency might appear contradictory, but it resolves the tension between the personal and the collective, between adhering to the "spirit of the male's authority" regarding the opinions expressed towards Israel by the men in their tribe, alongside the personal empowerment they achieved through the prolonged rehabilitation process with the help of the Ministry of Defense (Ben-Asher & Bokek-Cohen, 2017). As Palestinians, they are required to maintain a hesitant, restrained relationship with the State of Israel and its institutions, but this stance is not necessarily a result of their independent choice; rather, it is one of the hegemonic representations in the society they live in, shaped by historical, political, and social circumstances.

The issue of rights deeply concerned Sana, Faiza, and the other widows I met. The lack of translation of these rights from Hebrew to Arabic created a feeling that information about their entitlements was being withheld from them. Faiza spent nights translating word by word with a dictionary, groping in the dark to find information that was not readily accessible to her. The workers from the rehabilitation department were perceived as supportive and helpful, and all the widows noted their significant assistance in dealing with their husbands' families, in maintaining their right to open a private bank account where the compensations would be directed, and in handling issues with their children. Like many other widows, they responded to the rehabilitation department's invitation to join a group of Bedouin widows and shared that they found great value in these meetings, particularly in exchanging information about their rights and how to actualize them. However, the very fact that these meetings were held at the Ministry of Defense underscores the simultaneous co-existence regarding the question of the social sphere and the widows' connection to it — i.e., to the State of Israel and its Ministry of Defense, or to the Bedouin society — two entities between which there is ongoing conflict. Faiza stood and watched as border patrol soldiers, the unit in which her husband once served, demolished the house she had built for her son as he was about to get married.

As mentioned, Bedouin widows are expected to exhibit outward behavior of weakness, indicating a need for the protection of the family in general and male guardianship in particular. However, the economic status of IDF widows changes this picture because, unlike other Bedouin widows who must rely on family support, an IDF widow does not need to rely financially on the extended family. This change encourages the widow to develop a renewed worldview, both in terms of her own self-perception and her behavior within the family and tribe. All the widows in the study underwent a process of personal development following the acquisition of new information and ideas after their husband's death. This personal growth included economic independence and the ability to make personal and family decisions (Ben Asher and Bokek-Cohen, 2017).

Part of the difficulty in making and implementing decisions arises because these women make decisions for themselves, thereby challenging the deeply ingrained patriarchal perceptions of their traditional society. Such views are also called "social representations." The term "social representations" refers to the accepted norms within a group, understood as social constructs that are communicated among group members (Moscovici, 2001; 2007). These social representations serve as a sort of "guide to action" that the individual adopts as appropriate behaviors within the society in which they live (Ben-Asher, Wagner, & Orr, 2006).

Bedouin IDF widows expend considerable effort to avoid conflict or clashes between the hegemonic, traditional social representations and the new ones they adopt as independent women. They learn to drive in secrecy, sometimes with their faces veiled, strive to pursue education without leaving their residential areas, and outwardly, they continue to treat men with respectful deference. The circumstances in which Bedouin IDF widows find themselves open new, unfamiliar paths that do not require social acceptance. Their courage to act in ways suited to their individual realities leads them to adopt controversial viewpoints, even if they initially did not intend to challenge the prevailing perspectives. For instance, consider overseeing the construction of a house and having to direct male workers and craftsmen. Sana is aware that this role is considered unacceptable for women in Bedouin society: "If any man If a man permits me to supervise male laborers working on the house — then he's not the right man to be my husband. A Bedouin woman should not talk to the builder or do business at all. I did it." "She's a strong widow," the man who introduced me to her said with respect in his voice, which perhaps also masked his astonishment that a Bedouin widow could be relatively independent and manage her life without being entirely under male control. It seems that the road to acceptance of the Bedouin widow as independent and empowered within her society is still long.

The story of the Bedouin IDF widows — a very small community whose members live far apart from each other — reveals the social and emotional challenges they face. Their mourning practices and the ways they are regarded socially are deeply rooted in tradition and religion, but also in the political reality of national and military struggles. The monthly compensation provided by law for families of soldiers killed in action does not strengthen their sense of identification with the values of the State; rather, it merely formalizes the State's responsibility towards them. Bedouin widows face the need to rebuild their lives amidst a tangle of beliefs and conflicting messages. Despite the challenges, the economic independence gained through State compensation, coupled with their willingness to learn and grow with the support of rehabilitation counselors enables these women to reposition themselves within their patriarchal society and to become trailblazers for change.

However, it should be noted that Faiza and Sana, like the other interviewees in the study on widows, do not view themselves as societal representatives, or as champions of a social change. Instead, the widows see themselves as part of the extended family, the tribe, and the Bedouin-Palestinian society.

A shift in the Defense Ministry's policy towards a more culturally sensitive understanding bereavement, attuned to the complex reality filled with traditional, religious, and social messages, could aid the rehabilitation process and enhance post-traumatic growth through insights gained from the widows themselves. I personally have no doubt about the genuine intentions of the rehabilitation counselors, who are free from any racially motivated malice, to assist the Bedouin IDF widows. The potential contribution of listening to the voices of Faiza, Sana, and other young women, echoes in the poetry of Adonis:

Whenever I truly understand things,
I love more people.
As the space for speech contracts,
so too does the space for existence.
Your real victory is the constant shattering
of your triumphal arches.
(Adonis, 2013, p. 203)

Casting Light on The Shadow

Two of the women's stories cast light on issues that dwell in the shadows and vanish both from sight and public discourse: i.e., sexual assault within the Bedouin community and marital intimacy. Bedouin culture allocates a special place to shame as an "operational guide to behavior." Shame defines the boundaries of behavior, and crossing these limits can lead to ostracism from society. Two terms in Arabic describe shame: 'Eib (عيــب), an unacceptable act that brings shame to the perpetrator; and 'Aar (عــار), far more severe, as it not only shames the perpetrator but also their family, and thus demands the harshest of punishment, sometimes even murder (Haj-Yahia, 2000). These concepts are closely related, both enveloped in the heavy cloak of actions that are not only forbidden and due to the modesty demanded by traditional culture are also taboo to discuss. The grave threat to the victim's life enables cruel exploitation by perpetuating the assault, with the perpetrator assuming that the dire consequences of exposure — coupled with deep shame — would ensure that the offensive act, and particularly its victim, remain perpetually silent.

The stories of Hanan and Hiba touch on two sensitive issues — sexual assault and intimate marital relationships. These two women work actively to change public consciousness, while grappling with the societal norms that forbid bringing these silenced and marginalized topics into public discourse. They do so with courage and determination, employing strategies that circumvent the barriers of shame and dishonor.

Addressing Sexual Assault in Bedouin Society

In the conservative Arab-Bedouin society, family honor is paramount, and the revelation of sexual abuse severely undermines this value. The entire family's honor hinges on the woman's sexuality and modesty. Consequently, the Arab Bedouin man, who stands atop the social hierarchy, views preservation of family honor, i.e., essentially protecting the sexuality of daughters and wives, as one of his primary roles. "We do not sexually abuse our daughters," many Bedouin men claim. If pressed for an explanation, they say, "We guard our daughters and their honor so vigilantly that there is no chance a stranger would meet and sexually harass or assault them." But are these men truly depicting reality, or are they cloaking it in a thick layer of stereotypes and beliefs that prevent the light of truth from penetrating the dense fabric beneath which a different reality is buried?

Although the sexual assault of women, young girls, and children is not a new phenomenon, awareness of this aberrant behavior began to rise only in the 1980s, as evidenced by studies conducted on populations in Western societies (Doll, Koenig & Purcell, 2004). However, traditional societies still diligently deny the existence of this phenomenon among the ranks of their community even today. Despite the increase in the number of educated women in the Bedouin society, there is hardly any feminist discourse addressing autonomy, freedom, and the full rights of women over their bodies and lives. The outlook which espoused "her body, his control" to describe men's attitudes toward women's sexuality remains prevalent (Shlomi and Tzionit, 2015).

By its very nature, sexual assault occurs in secrecy, and concealment is an intrinsic part of the act. Professionals working in the field argue that the number of sexual assaults in the Bedouin society is vastly higher than what is reported. They claim that the taboo nature of the issue, combined with the insular family structure, greatly increases the risk of assault (Shlomi and Tzionit, 2015). Almost seven hundred requests for assistance are received annually by centers for victims of sexual violence in the Arab sector. It has been found that 65% of women and girls in the Bedouin sector who have suffered sexual abuse do not agree to file a police complaint about the assault (Natur and Lazovsky, 2010). Insaf Abu Shareb, who researches the lives of Arab and Bedouin women in Israel, refers to this as the "silence pact." Bedouin girls, teenagers, and women see violence as an unavoidable reality because the social norm dictates that a woman must not reveal acts of violence committed against her, nor complain about them to authorities. A woman who breaks this silence is likely to face ostracism and banishment by her family, and she may even be murdered for violating this duty of silence (Abu Shareb, 2013).

The moment of horror when Hanan heard that her daughter had been sexually assaulted is described in harsh words: "At that moment it was as if the sky had fallen on me, as if the earth had turned under me [...] I felt like I was falling into some deep, deep, deep pit." When a young girl is sexually assaulted, this is an assault of the 'Aar, the more severe type, and therefore the family typically has three options: if the offender is a family member, the daughter must be married off to him; if the offender is not a close family member, he should be murdered as revenge against him and his family; and the third option is to murder the victim to send a message as a deterrent to all other women.

Killing is a form of coping with the shame that the daughter is alleged to have caused the family. The first question Hanan asked the police officer when her daughter was brought to him was if anyone knew about the incident. His answer illustrates the severe sense of threat associated with the sexual assault injury of a young girl. The girl's uncle entered the station, handed the girl over to the police, and began banging his head against the wall. The Chief of Police, a Bedouin who also knows the cultural and social codes, said to the mother: "I understood that something terrible happened." Even he as a police officer, refrained from saying the words "sexual assault".

A fourth option available to the family after a sexual assault is providing treatment for the victim — an option that is hardly ever seen as legitimate: This path does not necessarily refer to treatment by a social worker or a psychologist, but rather to the treatment of traditional healers or religious clerics, who interpret the event as an act of "Maktub" (fate), and a test by God to examine the strength of their faith.

In Bedouin society, there are accounts of young women developing dissociative responses that involve detachment from emotions, sensations, memories, and thoughts, disconnection from physical reality, depression, and even sudden bouts of fainting, with no plausible explanation provided. Within their close community, these victims are often labeled as insane ("majnuneh"), and the behavioral changes are not linked to the profound emotional distress they endure, which arises from the sexual assault. The emotional therapy widely accepted in the Western world, remains almost entirely unimplemented in Bedouin society. Instead, there is often a preference to overlook the visible distress, hoping it will resolve on its own. In severe cases, families turn to traditional healers, whose treatments primarily involve potions and amulets. Hanan reflected on her own imagined sensation of free-falling during that initial moment of hearing about her daughter's attack: "A few weeks later, the downfall came for her. She [the daughter] began to sleep a lot, suffered from nightmares, [...] She became aggressive, stubborn, and irritable, and developed an obsessive compulsion for cleanliness and order. Anything out of place distressed her."

As an adult, the attempt at self-healing through faith in God went well with the mother. The experience of the foulness of the event transferred to her, and she dealt with it: "And precisely there, inside the deep pit, it was as if I heard a voice from the sky calling out, 'Be strong, cope'. I felt as if I had entered a cold shower that washed away all the filth from me. I felt that God was with me. He will not leave me, and I will not leave my daughter." The daughter also tried to hold on to her faith in God and began to hug the Koran and tuck it under her pillow. However, unlike her mother, in the daughter's case, this was not sufficient to alleviate her distress.

In cases of sexual abuse involving children, there isn't necessarily a clear narrative or a well-defined breaking point. Mechanisms of dissociation and silencing — hallmarks of sexual trauma — can significantly blur the ability to remember or articulate the story, especially when it involves childhood memories. Post-traumatic growth necessitates a story that carries meaning within the larger life narrative. In instances of sexual trauma, there is a need for testimony to understand the larger story. Meaning, the reconstruction of the abusive act, requires much more time and often unfolds, among other occasions, within the secure and protective environment of a therapeutic space.

Despite the suffering and distress experienced by the victim, appropriate treatment and support can enable positive development in the future, emerging from the acknowledgment of the harm and the ability to cope with the suffering. This growth includes the strong feelings of empathy and sensitivity that arise towards others who suffer and a renewed and fuller appreciation of life within the context of existential and spiritual questions. The treatment of sexual trauma is not a simple process. It requires staying with the victim in a space of pain by sharing a protected, intimate environment where they can express their difficult emotions (Zeligman, 2004). Treating sexual trauma, particularly in childhood and cases of incest, presents especially tough challenges for both therapist and client, however, the lack of appropriate care can lead to a high risk of repeated harm to both the victims themselves and others (Sadan, 2012).

Addressing sexual assault is thus imperative in any society, even those that silence the existence of the phenomenon. Hanan described the disagreement between her and her husband regarding psychological treatment for their daughter. He was opposed and did not understand how mere conversations with the child could help. Moreover, he believed such conversations could even be harmful: "My husband mocked me, saying, 'You are wasting your money and doing foolish things.'" While he was willing to compromise on their daughter receiving the traditional treatment he was familiar with, such as a session with the Sheikh, he took no steps to facilitate that treatment session.

Against the backdrop of Bedouin tradition, which is insular and denies the existence of such phenomena, Hanan's decision to act is not merely groundbreaking, but also a courageous personal move that could endanger her due to the possibility that someone might connect her public efforts to a personal experience. It is possible her status as an educated woman, a responsible nurse at the hospital, and a religious woman respected and esteemed by Bedouin leaders and family heads that prevented an open backlash against her initiative. Hanan's imposing personal presence, which no one can overlook, makes her a leader, even if much of her work still takes place behind closed doors (as evidence of this — I am even prohibited from disclosing her name).

"No One Talks About It:"
Wedding Night Guidance for Grooms and Brides

The World Health Organization defines human sexuality as:

An inner energy that propels us to seek love, touch, warmth, and intimacy. Sexuality influences our thoughts, feelings, and interpersonal interactions. Given its significant impact on our physical and mental health, the right to express our sexuality is included as a fundamental aspect of an individual's right to health (Alasad-Alhuzail, 2016).

It appears that even today, this fundamental right is not realized within the Bedouin society. In Bedouin culture, a couple's relationship is defined as a bond between a man and a woman, anchored in social and religious recognition. Alasad-Alhuzail studied three generations of Bedouin women and found that for the middle generation, the stability of the couple's relationship largely depended on the woman's behavior, which sustained and enhanced their partnership. This was the case, despite the fact that the marriages in the study were typically arranged by families, with many couples not meeting each other prior to being married. It appears that the women embrace a closely-knit relational system where dependency between partners forms part of a dialogue intended to evolve throughout their shared lives. As one woman from the middle generation put it, "A relationship is like a flock and a shepherd. The man is the shepherd – he knows nothing about his flock. Everything depends on her" (p. 109). From a slightly distant perspective on her words, it might seem that although the woman tries to describe her activeness in practical life and to build a family system in which the man would struggle without her, metaphorically, she sees herself as a sheep and the man as the shepherd who controls (at least) her. Among women of the third generation, those in their twenties and early thirties, a relationship is a refuge from stifling family life, a place where they hope to be freer in their emotions and thoughts and to have a partner for their inner, personal world (Abu-Rbia-Queder, 2005; Alasad-Alhuzail, 2016).

The absence of discourse on sexuality in Bedouin society is an extension of the prevailing attitudes towards sexual education in general. In a focus group I conducted on this subject with six Bedouin female students aged 26 to 34, from the generation Alasad-Alhuzail calls "the third generation," it became clear that none of them had received guidance on the intimate aspects of the relationship between men and women before marriage. Their knowledge came from hints dropped by older sisters or from friends who had married before them, and primarily focused on the anticipated pain they should experience on their wedding night. Here is a part of the conversation held with these young women, who describe this better than any scholarly description could:[18]

By the end of ninth grade, I knew nothing ... no one had told me anything. My older sisters would talk among themselves when they argued with their husbands, but never about what happened in their intimate lives. At school, apart from one biology lesson, nothing was discussed. There was a newspaper in the library that we secretly read about marital problems between a husband and a wife. I got married at eighteen and a half to my cousin. He was a Bedouin my age. On our first night together, I didn't really understand what was happening. It was scary. I had never seen a naked man before. I closed my eyes out of fear and pain. Men want what they want. Sometimes it's like rape. If he wants, you have to comply. My husband was cold as ice. He never thought to let me enjoy being together. Sometimes I was disgusted by him. After he was with me, he would just go to sleep, and I would cry all night. I felt like a prostitute. He didn't talk to me at all and simply sought to satisfy himself. (Suha)

From my experience, no one talks about it, not even my mother. If you ask your sister, perhaps she'll tell you something. Before the wedding, I received no information at all. Everyone only talked to me about the wedding itself —

---

18 The discussion is presented with consent of the participants and under pseudonyms.

the party, the clothes, and the gifts. After the wedding night, my husband's friends asked him how it went. He is expected to say it was fine. (Shifa)

Girlfriends talk, saying "This and that will happen," but without knowing the truth. Sisters and aunts say that the first night will be tough and that you need to get through the first time and move on. I know a daughter of a friend whose husband raped her. (Wafa)

When I was in tenth grade, one of the girls left and got married. During a visit back to school, she shared with the girls what happens in the bedroom. My friend and I were so mortified that we got out of there. (Huda)

Mother told me that I needed to be good to my husband, but she didn't say a thing about what would happen. Either she was embarrassed or thought the school had taught me. I searched on the Internet. What I read scared me even more. I was curious, but ashamed to ask my mom what I wanted to know. It's a delicate subject. (Nadin)

Based on the women's accounts in this conversation, it was clear they had not received any formal Sex education in school. Information on sexuality was conveyed to the young adolescents only by their sisters or mothers, and even then, it was heavily censored. This information primarily revolved around the passive role that women are expected to adopt in intimate relationships, especially on their wedding night.

Michel Foucault, in his 1996 book *"The History of Sexuality,"* illustrates how discourse on sexuality serves as a regulatory mechanism that shapes the "normal" boundaries of sexual practice. According to Foucault, the silencing power of this discourse reveals regulatory and supervisory practices through prohibitions and sexual definitions. Feminist thinkers have extended Foucault's ideas from a starting point of the patriarchal suppression of women by men (Rodriguez-Garcia, 2015). Hiba emphasizes in her remarks that she is not a feminist. It is unclear whether she is deeply familiar with the socio-philosophical concepts of various feminist currents, such as liberal, radical, and postmodern feminism. To her, feminism appears to be the antithesis of religion and tradition. She declares herself to be a religious woman, working to change the status quo with a deep belief rooted in a religious worldview based on Quranic verses. Likewise, Hiba utilizes books on sexual and marital guidance — choosing those with a traditional-conservative tone to support the desired change in marital relationships built by the couple.

Change does not occur in a vacuum. The young Bedouin women described the internet as an accessible source of knowledge today for young people in all areas, including guidance on intimate relationships. However, from their words, it appears that this "objective" source actually heightens their anxiety rather than diminishing it. "Is there another woman who guides brides and grooms like you?" I asked Hiba, and she replied that she knew of no one else. It appears that without reinforcement of her efforts to create a network of bridal and groom guides and to establish a clear professional identity, her leadership initiative might remain a local, singular anecdote, despite its great significance and tremendous potential.

Hiba's intuitive initiative recalls the words of the French-born American writer, of Cuban descent, Anaïs Nin (1903-1977), who was influenced by feminist currents: "And the day came when the risk to remain tight in a bud was more painful than the risk it took to blossom." Hiba scatters flowers in the bedroom, lights small candles that emit a pleasant fragrance, arranges a set of white pajamas for the bride, and then returns home. As she goes to sleep, she hopes that the guidance the bride and groom received close to or on their wedding day will allow them to experience the pleasure of being together in their first intimate encounter without pain, fear, or humiliation.

Leadership Behind Closed Doors

The belief in the individual's right to free choice, independence, privacy, and gender equality does not align with the values of the traditional Arab family, which are rooted in collectivism. Such a worldview highlights values like the importance of hierarchical relationships, mutual dependence, harmony, maintaining a good reputation, as well as a commitment to family and close relatives (Jraisi, 2012; Dvir, Buchbinder & Siman, 2006; 2014). Anyone aspiring to lead change in Bedouin society must deeply understand its customs, beliefs, traditions, and thought processes.

The understanding that intervention strategies in any field must be tailored to the unique characteristics and context of a society and its culture is not new, as they influence an individual's perspective and behavior (for a comprehensive review, see Nijem-Akthilat, Ben Rabi, and Sabo-Lal, 2018). Practitioners who enter traditional Arab society armed with academic and practical knowledge acquired through a Western lens may struggle to communicate effectively. They often lack the necessary tools to drive change from within the community, or the ability to utilize local resources.

Zoabi (2013) believes that practitioners from the same cultural background as the patient also encounter similar challenges and must devise strategies to overcome them. These conflicts arise because the practitioners are trained in a profession developed in the West. Therefore, Zoabi suggests that in such cases, intra-cultural interventions (*intervention culturalintra*) should be employed, which are derived from and evolve within the shared culture of both the practitioner and the client.

Hanan and Hiba are leaders, and their leadership is built upon a profound familiarity with their society and culture. However, if ever they were ever formally acknowledged as "leaders," they would likely shun the title as if it might impede their efforts, preferring to remain behind the scenes. These women focus on action rather than on their leadership status, which manifests in the shaded and hidden areas of Bedouin society and culture. The spotlight could disrupt the transformations they facilitate behind closed doors (Amit, Popper, Gal, Maman, and Lisk, 2008). They do not appear on public stages but operate with great caution, fearing that traditional forces might undermine their initiatives. Their leadership exists within a social context and is driven by a personal vision that each has developed in her field of work, also arising from a keen awareness of societal barriers in general, and specifically, those related to women's status in Bedouin society. Employing their innate wisdom, along with the resources and strategies they acquired and strengthened through their higher education, they seek to identify and address the painful areas of their society — "How can one understand an issue whose existence is altogether denied?" Hanan wonders.

Both Hiba and Hanan are driven to create change from a deep-seated identity as observant, religious women. While they consider feminism an idea for future generations, they are unwilling to let the forces of darkness continue to dominate the life of the Bedouin woman: "Our women have been birthing like sheep all their lives," a man railed against Hanan after she demanded follow-up care for his pregnant wife, but she remained undeterred. They are not seeking roles defined by someone else, but are acting out of a profound personal and social commitment. They do not need a top-down action plan because their existence is deeply rooted in Bedouin society, in the beauty of their traditions and culture, and in its darkest shadows: "I take the traditional wisdom and implement it on the ground," Heba describes her approach. They use verses from the Quran and proudly present them to help women recognize their own value and rights: "Nowhere is it written that a woman is like a rag," Hiba challenges.

Research on informal leadership globally (for example, Feldman & Stall, 2004; Robnett, 1997) shows that informal leaders are often women from marginalized social groups, and the leadership model they employ significantly differs from the conventional model of authoritative and hierarchical leadership. Their primary strength lies in their ability to operate within the local community and to serve as a bridge between the community and the political or religious establishments. Often, their charismatic leadership is built on the emotional connections they develop with community members rather than on formal authority (Davidovich-Epstein, 2005).

Hanan's story reflects a leadership aimed at influencing the entire Bedouin population in the Negev, not just the local community. Hiba, in contrast, operates as a local leader within her neighborhood using a "word of mouth" approach. Both women are not part of the elected political leadership or business elite. Hiba is active in neighborhood organizations, while Hanan engages with civil society organizations.

Does a local leader who emerges from the grassroots truly have the autonomy and genuine capacity to influence the residents? Can leadership that operates behind the scenes truly make a lasting impact, and can such influence be sustained in the future without the direct and active involvement of those same leaders?

What is the source of Hanan and Hiba's power? Are they capable of impacting the existing realities of Bedouin society even under conditions of shadowed leadership (i.e., behind the scenes)? Through her activities in a social organization that aids victims of sexual assault, will Hanan succeed in bringing Bedouin society to recognize the existence of the phenomenon of sexual abuse of minors and take moral and institutional responsibility to protect the victims, taking care of them and building new norms for intervention (in addition to implementing programs for community awareness on the subject)?

Will Hiba, who operates independently in the field with the same intensity that enabled her to establish an improvised neighborhood community center in the past, be able to raise public awareness regarding the importance of pre-marital counseling and change the prevailing perception which considers intimate contact between the partners of a couple as a kind of "conquest" that often, in practice, becomes an act of rape on the wedding night? Will Hiba's efforts evolve into significant change within Bedouin society? Will the social and educational responsibility to guide couples as they transition toward a new developmental stage in their lives be embraced as a norm, similar, for example, to practices observed within the ultra-Orthodox community?

In order to explore these questions, it is crucial to understand the field of action, the realm hidden from the public eye, and the world in which these leaders operate. Yet, it is important to note that intuitive leadership alone is not sufficient; effective leadership generally also requires learned skills and knowledge. The attitudinal shift and beneficial alternative that Hiba provided to dozens of couples on their wedding night is proof that seeds of change can sprout in near darkness, surreptitiously, and in the middle of the night, in places where ancient traditions remain unmentioned. Yet, it is doubtful whether society can cast the responsibility for socio-cultural change on one individual, even if that individual is the innovator. This, Hiba's approach, represents a significant shift in male-female relations, placing a focus on equality and respect for the fundamental right of every person, man or woman, to safeguard their body and derive joy from an intimate, sensitive, and considerate connection. Conversely, the fact that Hanan operates within a social organization, together with partners, enhances the likelihood that her messages will proliferate and have an impact. A Bedouin proverb states, "He who wants to lead the camels must widen his doorway."

The recognition of the need for social repair is a product of neo-liberal views that do not disavow tradition and religion, though they do oppose ignorance and darkness. This is where individual initiative needs to pervade the community, and from there to organizations and institutions, until it becomes anchored as part of the new culture that the Bedouin society seeks to adopt.

Epilogue

My parents arrived in the Negev on the night following Yom Kippur, between October 5th and 6th of 1946, participating in the most extensive settlement operation in the land of Israel before the creation of the state. Eleven new settlements ("The Eleven Points") were established during that single transformative night, which eventually blossomed into thriving communities, dramatically altering the nation's landscape. At that time, the Negev was not deserted; it was inhabited by tens of thousands of Bedouins whose ancestors had lived on this arid soil for generations. During the scorching summers, these nomadic families were forced to migrate northward with their herds in search of pasture. As autumn arrived, before the sparse rains began to turn the hills green, the Bedouins returned to the hillside and the expanses of grey, yellow, and brown they had left months before. Two years after that fateful night of the "Eleven Points", as Israel's Declaration of Independence was proclaimed, the British withdrew from the land, leaving us as neighbors.

The Bedouins traditionally planted Drimia Aphylla between their fields. The tall stately rows of Drimia Aphylla, with stems boasting their unique beauty and blossoms that unfurl day after day in neatly organized tiers from bottom to top, clearly delineate the boundaries between land plots. These land demarcations were preserved from season to season by the bitter taste of the Drimia Aphylla bulbs, which at summer's end deterred even the hungriest sheep from eating them. Each plot was akin to its own distinct territory, having belonged to one of the tribe's families for generations. To an outsider, the plots may seem indistinguishable, but a Bedouin tending to his land would always discern and appreciate its unique character.

The stories of Kawkab, Amal, Adel, Faiza, Sana, Hanan, and Hiba are as diverse as the plots of land separated by the hardy

Drimia bulbs. Their life narratives and ways of navigating their surroundings resemble Drimia blossoms and its bitter bulbs.One who observes these women witnesses not only their unique experiences, characterized by clearly defined boundaries, but also their blossoming and maturation as they confront the challenges interwoven into their lives. However, at the same time, the women recognize the bitter cultural realities embedded within their existence. At the roots of the tradition lie foundations that sustain a visibly oppressive life system, depriving women of the fundamental right to determine their own destinies. The inherited bitterness, silently transmitted from mother to daughter reflects the hardships of life, symbolized by the Drimia bulb hidden deep in the soil. We, as listeners and observers of the expanse revealed before us, see the boundary between the various personal stories, each distinct from the next, and the traces of time that leave their mark on each one. We also discern the heavy, bitter, and hidden cost they seldom voice directly, fearing it might destroy their lives. Yet, if our gaze extends past this space to the horizon, we will capture the beginnings of a deep tilling, or turning of the soil in the social field—the field in which these women, like their ancestors, toiled with simple tools, hoping their efforts would yield new crops.

However, observers of Bedouin society will always see the aggregate, reminiscent of the expansive, towering desert dunes. The collection of women's accounts I heard, (a fraction of which are detailed in this book), is comparable to gathering grains of sand within a vast dune. I carefully cup my hands, cradling some the of insights gleaned, and gaze intently, fascinated by the material from which they were formed, and by the power that is concealed behind their profound subordination to the patriarchal society, its laws, and its commands. Afterward, I spread my fingers and return the observations to their original location. Nature will take its course. It is far more challenging to observe the structural changes caused by the delicate shifting of sand grains within the enormous mass to which they belong collectively. Those who listen closely can hear a gentle whisper as they move. The Bedouin women, veiled beneath the hijabs cascading down to their sandals, blurring the lines of their bodies and under headscarves tightly pinned to their heads with sparkling brooches, are the secret architects of significant change. I believe this cautious and gentle movement is happening across the limestone hills, amidst the recognized and the unrecognized villages. This movement, hidden from sight, involving the women described in this book and others working throughout the Negev's new towns and unrecognized villages, will one day coalesce like a torrential storm in the desert, arriving just moments after the echoing roar of the stones swept within it, like a mighty wind set to transform reality.

> The desert requires a geologist
> to decipher its contours, and, at the very least,
> one who can read the future from a palm or the past.
> (Yehuda Amichai, 2015)

I know that any interpretation of the desert's defining contours is destined to be fleeting, lasting only until the next wind sweeps through and sculpts them anew.

Three times while writing this book, the hills between my home and theirs were painted in the resilient yellow of chrysanthemums; three times, all the vegetation withered and dried out under the sweltering summer sun, leaving the hills exposed and tormented. I pause my writing, gaze toward the horizon, and see nothing but emptiness. Since the day I was born, I have recognized and been familiar with the winds blowing from the distant deserts and stinging us with the fine grains of sand they carry with them. I pray that it will only be these desert winds that strike us, and not any other, more sinister storm. With those winds heralding the seasonal changes of the arid Negev, we have learned to live in peace.

Acknowledgments

For me, writing this book was a fascinating journey of reinterpreting the familiar yet enigmatic essence of human existence. Throughout this journey, I had many collaborators for whom I am deeply grateful. Their generosity in sharing their knowledge and joining me in weaving the delicate and intricate threads of personal stories and academic insights was invaluable. Foremost among the collaborators in creating this book were the Bedouin women who courageously opened their hearts and shared with me the stories of their lives, offering new insights, and revealing their challenges.

Thank you to the graduates of the Mandel Center for Leadership in the Negev's leadership programs from the Arab Bedouin community, who helped me connect with some of the women whose leadership is often unseen and for whom the paths to communication with them require trust and connection through a prior acquaintance. My gratitude also extends to the Mandel Foundation Israel and Dr. Adi Nir Sagi, Director of the Mandel Center in the Negev, who supported and encouraged me to deepen my engagement and personal learning about the lives of the young Bedouin women.

I am grateful to the publishing team at the Mofet Institute who first released the book in Hebrew (2020), and to Minerva Publishing who released Kawkab in Arabic (2023). The responses I received from the young Bedouin women who read the book in both Hebrew and Arabic encouraged me to bring their stories to an English-speaking audience outside of Israel.

Thank you to the Mifal HaPayis Council for Arts & Sciences for finding this book worthy of a support grant for its publication in the category of reference and research books. Thank you, as well, to Achva College, its President Prof. Yifat Biton, and the college's Research Authority who assisted me in the publication of the book.

Translation of this book into English was entrusted to the professional hands of Amy Erani, who with great sensitivity and discernment successfully navigated between three languages: Arabic, the language of the book's heroines, intertwining their personal stories with expressions and concepts unique to Arab culture and language; Hebrew, in which the book was originally written; and English, into which the book was translated. This task is a true art form, demanding a deep understanding of linguistic expressions that embody a diverse array of unique cultural meanings.

Heartfelt thanks to the esteemed Prof. Ruth Kark, who encouraged the translation of this book into English and provided invaluable guidance with her extensive experience.

Thank you to Prof. Yitzhak Reiter, who supported the publication of this book in English and offered invaluable academic consultation throughout the translation process, greatly enriching the work with his rich expertise in the field.

Lastly, I must thank my family, whose lives are interwoven with mine: my sister Tamar, broad in horizon and knowledge, has been a supportive and attentive conversational partner. I could share with her the experiences of discovery and initial thoughts before they matured into structured knowledge; my grown children — Noam, Ella, and Inbal — who encouraged my creative endeavors that diverged from the academic articles I had previously published. Finally, I wish to express my gratitude to Alex, with whom I shared countless daily conversations, thoughts, dilemmas, and questions throughout the process of writing this book.

I dedicate this book to the courageous Bedouin women, whose actions, even if only partially visible, inspire awe and admiration.

BIBLIOGRAPHY

Sources in English

Abu-Bader, S., & Gottlieb, D. (2013). Poverty, education, and employment among the Arab Bedouin in Israel. In V. Berenger & F. Bresson (Eds.), *Poverty and social exclusion around the Mediterranean Sea* (pp. 213-245). New York: Springer.

Abu-Lughod, L. (2013). *Do Muslim women need saving?* Cambridge, MA: Harvard University Press.

Abu-Rabia-Queder, S. (2017). "The paradox of professional marginality among Arab-Bedouin women". *Sociology*, 51(5), pp. 1084-1100.

Abu-Rabia-Queder, S., & Arar, K. (2011). "Gender and higher education in different national spaces: Female Palestinian students attending Israeli and Jordanian universities". *Compare*, 41(3), pp. 353-370.

Abu-Rabia-Queder, S., & Karplus, Y. (2013). "Regendering space and reconstructing identity: Bedouin women's trans-local mobility into Israeli-Jewish institutions of higher education". *Gender, Place & Culture*, 20(4), pp. 470-486.

Abu-Rabia-Queder, S., Morris, A., & Ryan, H. (2018). "The economy of survival: Bedouin women in unrecognized villages". *Journal of Arid Environments*, 149, pp. 80-88.

Abu-Rabia-Queder, S., & Weiner-Levy, N. (2013). "Between local and foreign structures: Exploring the agency of Palestinian women in Israel". *Social Politics*, 20(1), pp. 88-108.

Alsraiha, K. (2020). "From a boss to a leader? Transformations of representational leadership in the Arab Bedouin minority in Israel". *Journal of Muslim Minority Affairs*, 40(2), pp. 271-283.

Arar, K., & Shapira, T. (2016). "Hijab and principalship: The interplay between belief systems, educational management, and gender among Arab Muslim women in Israel." *Gender and Education*, 28(7), pp. 851-866.

Ben-Asher, S. (2016). "Bedouin children and their reality perceptions of the war". *Journal of Muslim Minority Affairs,* 36(4), pp. 1–18.

Ben-Asher, S. (Oct. 2018). "Seeing and not understanding: When the media brings children social representations of war". *Comprender Actuar Transcender Journal,* 1, pp. 75-96 (Co Act Journal).

Ben-Asher, S., & Bokek-Cohen, Y. (2017). "Clashing identities in the military bereavement of a minority group: The case of Bedouin IDF widows in Israel". *Papers on Social Representations,* 26(1), pp. 1-7.

Ben-Asher, S., & Bokek-Cohen, Y. (2019). "Liminality and emotional labor among war widows in Israel". *Culture & Psychology.* doi: 10.1177/1354067X19828981.

Ben-Asher, S. & Lebel, U. (2010). "Social structure vs. self-rehabilitation: IDF widows forming an intimate relationship in the sociopolitical discourse." *Journal of Comparative Research in Anthropology and Sociology,* 1(2), pp. 39–60.

Ben-Asher, S., Sabar Ben-Yehoshua, N., & Albador, A. (2020). "'Neither here nor there': Flattening, omission, silencing, and silence in the construction of narrative identity among Islamic teenage girls who Jewish schools". *Israel Affairs,* 26(1).

Ben-Asher, S., Wagner, W., & Orr, E. (2006). "Thinking groups: Rhetorical enactment of collective identity in three Israeli Kibbutzim". *Asian Journal of Social Psychology,* 9(2), pp. 112-122.

Bokek-Cohen, Y., & Ben-Asher, S. (2018). "The double exclusion of Bedouin war widows". *International Journal on Minority and Group Rights,* 25(1), pp. 112-131.

Buchbinder, E., & Siman, L. (2014). "Between the cultural and the professional in management: The experiences of Arab public welfare agency managers in Israel". *Journal of Social Work,* 14(4), pp. 341-359.

Deci, E. L., & Ryan, R. M. (2012). "Motivation, personality, and development within embedded social contexts: An overview of self-determination theory". In R. M. Ryan (Ed.), *The Oxford Handbook of Human Motivation* (pp. 85-107). Oxford: Oxford University Press.

Doll, L. S., Koenig, L. J., & Purcell, D. W. (2004). "Child sexual abuse and adult sexual risk: Where are we now?", in L. J. Koenig, L. S. Doll, A. O'Leary & W. Pequegnat (Eds.), *From child sexual abuse to adult sexual risk: Trauma, revictimization, and intervention* (pp. 3-10). Washington, DC: American Psychological Association.

Dwairy, M., & El-Jamil, F. (2008). "Counseling Arab and Muslim Clients". *Counseling across cultures*, pp. 147-160.

Feldman, M. R., & Stall, S. (2004). *The dignity of resistance: Women residents' activism in Chicago public housing.* Cambridge: Cambridge University Press.

Finkelstein, M. A. (2010). "Individualism/collectivism: Implications for the volunteer process". *Social Behavior and Personality: an international journal,* 38(4), pp. 445-452.

Geertz, C. (1983). *Local knowledge: Further essays in interpretive anthropology.* New York: Basic Books.

Geertz, C. (1984). "Distinguished lecture: Anti anti-relativism". *American Anthropologist,* 86(2), pp. 263-278.

Geertz, C. (2008). *Local knowledge: Further essays in interpretive anthropology.* New York: Basic books.

Ghanim, H. (2009). "Poetics of disaster: Nationalism, gender, and social change among Palestinian poets in Israel after Nakba." *International Journal of Politics, Culture, and Society,* 22(1), pp. 23-39.

Gribiea, A., Ben-Asher, S., & Kupferberg, I. (2019). "Silencing and silence in Negev Bedouin students' narrative discourse." *Israel Affairs,* 25(4), pp. 617-634. Retrieved from https://www.tandfonline.com/doi/abs/10.1080/13537 121.2019.1626080.

Haj-Yahia, M. M. (2000). "Wife abuse and battering in the sociocultural context of Arab society." *Family Process,* 39(2), pp. 237-255.

Hochschild, A. R. (2003). *The commercialization of intimate life: Notes from home and work.* Berkeley: University of California Press.

Kedar, A., Amara, A., & Yiftachel, O. (2018). *Emptied lands: A legal geography of Bedouin rights in the Negev.* Stanford: Stanford University Press.

Kark, R. (2024*). The Negev & The Bedouin: Nomadism Living Areas, and the Issue of Land, 1800-1967,* Israel Academic Press.

Lance, J. (1990). "What the stranger brings: The social dynamics of fieldwork". *History in Africa,* 17, pp. 335-339. doi: 10.2307/3171822.

Lebel, U. (2011). "Militarism versus security? The double-bind of Israel's culture of bereavement and hierarchy of sensitivity to loss". *Mediterranean Politics,* 6(3), pp. 365-384.

Mahmood, S. (2005). *Politics of piety: The Islamic revival and the feminist subject.* Princeton, NJ: Princeton University Press.

Malkinson, R. E., Rubin, S. S. E., & Witztum, E. E. (2000). *Traumatic and nontraumatic loss and bereavement: Clinical theory and practice.* Madison: Psychosocial Press.

Marbley, A. F., & Bonner, F. A. (2007). "Interfacing culture-specific pedagogy with counseling: A proposed diversity training model for preparing preservice teachers for diverse learners". *Multicultural Education,* 14(3), pp. 8-16.

Meler, T. (2014). "Currencies of social support: Israeli-Palestinian single mothers in their families and communities". *Comparative Sociology,* 13(3), pp. 315-334. doi:10.1163/15691330-12341307.

Meler, T. (2015). "'I do what I please, but even so, I see a psychologist': Palestinian divorced and widowed mothers in Israel". *Journal of Middle East Women's Studies,* 11(3), pp. 306-324.

Moscovici, S. (2001). "Why a theory of social representation?" In K. Deaux & G. Philogene (Eds.), *Representation of the social: Bridging theoretical traditions* (pp. 8-37). Oxford: Blackwell.

Ogbu, J. U. (2004). "Collective identity and the burden of "Acting White" in black history, community, and education". *The Urban Review,* 36, pp. 1-40.

Ogbu, J. U., & Simons, H. D. (1998). "Voluntary and involuntary minorities: A cultural-ecological theory of school performance with some implications for education". *Anthropology and Education Quarterly,* 29, pp. 155-188.

Popper-Giveon, A., & Al-Krenawi, A. (2010). "Women as healers; women as clients: The encounter between traditional Arab women healers and their clients". *Culture, Medicine, and Psychiatry,* 34(3), pp. 468-499.

Robnett, B. (1997). *How long? How long?* New York: Oxford University Press.

Rogers, M. (2012). "Contextualizing theories and practices of bricolage research". *The Qualitative Report,* 17(48), pp. 1-17.

Rubin, L. (2017). Islamic political activism among Israel's Negev Bedouin population. *British Journal of Middle eastern studies,* 44(3), pp. 429-446.

Ryan, R. M., & Deci, E. L. (2000). "Intrinsic and extrinsic motivations: Classic definitions and new directions". *Contemporary Educational Psychology,* 25(1), pp. 54-67.

Savaya, R. (1998). "The under-use of psychological services by Israeli Arabs: An examination of the roles of negative attitudes and the use of alternative sources of help". *International Social Work,* 41(2), pp. 195-209.

Silverman, P. R., & Nickman, S. L. (1996). "Children's construction of their dead parents". In D. Klass, P. R. Silverman & S. L. Nickman (Eds.), *Continuing bonds: New understandings of grief* (pp. 73-86). Washington: Taylor and Francis.

Simmel, G. (1950). "The Stranger". In K. H. Wolff (Ed.), *The sociology of Georg Simmel* (pp. 402-408). New York: Free Press.

Spector-Mersel, G. (2011). "Mechanisms of selection in claiming narrative identities: A model for interpreting narratives". Qualitative Inquiry, 17(2), pp. 172-185.

Yiftachel, O., Roded, B., & Kedar, A. (2016). "Between rights and denials: Bedouin Indigeneity in the Negev/Naqab". *Environment and Planning A: Economy and Space,* 48(11), pp. 2129-2161.

Sources in Hebrew   **מקורות בעברית**

אבו־רביעה־קווידר, ס' (2005). מתמודדות מתוך שוליות: שלושה דורות של נשים בדוואיות בנגב. בתוך ה' דהאן־כלב, נ' ינאי ונ' ברקוביץ (עורכות), *נשים בדרום: מרחב, פריפריה מיגדר* (עמ' 86–108). קריית שדה־בוקר: מכון בן־גוריון לחקר ישראל.

אבו־רביעה־קווידר, ס' (2017). *זהות מעמדית בהתהוות: פרופסיונליות פלסטיניות בנגב.* ירושלים: מאגנס.

אבו שארב, א' (2013). *קשר השתיקה: אלימות במשפחה נגד נשים ערביות־בדוואיות בנגב.* תל אביב: עמותת איתך מעכי – משפטניות למען צדק חברתי.

אגבריה, ס"ס (2015). מאמר דעה: נישואי בוסר בחברה הערבית. *נקודת מפגש, 9,* עמ' 12–16.

אדוניס (2013). *מפתח פעולות הרוח* (ר' שניר, תרגום, מבוא והערות). תל אביב: קשב לשירה.

אייל, י' ותירוש, א' (2018). מדדים חברתיים־כלכליים של האוכלוסייה הבדואית בנגב. דמ־774-18. מכון מאיירס־ג'וינט־ברוקדייל.

אלאסד־אלהוזייל, נ' (2016). *כשהצל גדל סימן שהשמש שוקעת: חייהן של נשים בדוואיות בראי השינויים.* תל אביב: רסלינג.

אלבדור, א' (2018). *השפעת הלימודים בבית ספר יהודי על התפתחות וגיבוש הזהות האישית של תלמידות בדוואיות.* (עבודת גמר לקבלת תואר "מוסמך בייעוץ חינוכי"). המכללה האקדמית לחינוך ע"ש קיי.

אל־בוח'ארי, מ' (2013). *צחיח אל־בח'ארי: אל־ג'אמע אל־מסנד א־צחיח.* [האוסף המהימן המאושר המקוצר של ענייניו של הנביא מוחמד עליו השלום וקורותיו]. קהיר: דאר אלפג'ר לא־תראת'.

אלמגור־לוטן, א', בר, א' ולוי, ש' (2010). *היום הבינלאומי למיגור העוני: לקט נתונים.* ירושלים: הכנסת, מרכז המחקר והמידע.

אלמסי, א' (2023). נתונים על אוכלוסיית הבדואים בנגב. הכנסת, מרכז המחקר והמידע. http://www.knesset.gov.il/mmm

אלפסי-הנלי, מ' (2016). בדואים עם מוגבלות בדרום הארץ: גודל האוכלוסיה, מאפייני רקע ותעסוקה. משרד הכלכלה והתעשייה, מחקר וכלכלה.

אלקרינאוי, ע' וסלונים-נבו, ו' (2005). נישואין פוליגמיים ומונוגמיים: השפעתם על מצבן הנפשי והחברתי של נשים בדואיות-ערביות. בתוך ר' לב-ויזל, ג' צוויקל ונ' ברק (עורכות), "שמרי נפשך": בריאות נפשית בקרב נשים בישראל (עמ' 149–167). באר שבע: אוניברסיטת בן-גוריון בנגב.

אמית, ק', פופר, מ', גל, ר', ממן, ת' וליסק, א' (2008). על התפתחות מנהיגים: מחקר השוואתי בין מנהיגים ללא מנהיגים. מגמות, 3, עמ' 464–488.

בן אשר, ס' (2001). מפגש הייצוגים החברתיים של החברה המזרחית עם הייצוגים החברתיים של החברה המערבית בעבודת היועצים החינוכיים במגזר הבדואי. הייעוץ החינוכי, י, עמ' 187–203.

בן אשר, ס' (2016). השפה כראי המציאות השבורה: תפיסת ילדים בדווים את המלחמה. עיונים בשפה וחברה, 8(1–2), עמ' 64–90.

בן אשר, ס' ובוקק-כהן, י' (2017). שכול מודר: תפיסות השכול של אלמנות צה"ל הבדואיות. חברה ורווחה, לז(4), עמ' 805–830.

בן אשר, ס' ומרעי, ו' (2012). עבודה קבוצתית עם סבתות בדואיות המטפלות בנכדיהן. מקבץ: כתב העת הישראלי לטיפול קבוצתי, 17(1), עמ' 69–85.

בר-דוד, י' (2003). אני גר בשכירות בבית שלי: מעולמם של סטודנטים ערבים באוניברסיטה אחת בישראל – סיור אתנוגרפי (עבודת גמר לקבלת תואר "מוסמך למדעי הרוח והחברה"). אוניברסיטת בן-גוריון בנגב.

ברכאת, א' (2018). נשים בחברות פטריארכליות נאבקות להשיג השכלה: המקרה של נשים דרוזיות בישראל. מגמות, נג(2), עמ' 83–106.

בר שלום, י' (2011). מחשבות על המחקר האתנוגרפי. שבילי מחקר, 17, עמ' 94–101.

גאנם, ע' (2007). שייכות אך שונות: הבניית זהות בקרב פלסטינאיות אזרחיות ישראל בוגרות בתי ספר יהודיים-ישראליים (עבודת גמר לקבלת תואר "מוסמך במדעי הרוח והחברה"). אוניברסיטת בן-גוריון בנגב.

ג'ראיסי, ע' (2012). טיפול פסיכוסוציאלי בחברה הערבית. בתוך מ' חובב, א' לונטל וי' קטן (עורכים), עבודה סוציאלית בישראל (עמ' 527–559). תל אביב: הקיבוץ המאוחד.

דוידוביץ-אפשטיין, ר' (2005). דפוסי התקשרות והיבטים תוך-נפשיים וביר-אישיים של מנהיגות. *מפגש לעבדה חינוכית סוציאלית*, 21, עמ' 115–135.

דוירי, מ' (2006). סוגיות בהערכה פסיכולוגית של מטופלים מחברות קולקטיביות: המקרה הערבי. *שיחות*, כ"א(1), עמ' 26–32.

דרורי-גוהר, ל' (עורכת). (2011). *תורת טיפול העובד הסוציאלי במשפחות שכולות*. תל אביב: משרד הביטחון, אגף משפחות והנצחה.

המועצה להשכלה גבוהה (2017). קידום ההשכלה הגבוהה בחברה הבדואית. https://tinyurl.com/y36brlm7

וייסבלאי, א' (2017). *חינוך בחברה הבדואית בנגב: תמונת מצב*. ירושלים: הכנסת, מרכז המחקר והמידע.

ויניגר, א' (2013). *נתונים על מערכת החינוך במגזר הבדואי*. ירושלים: הכנסת, מרכז המחקר והמידע.

זועבי, ח' (2013). *הקשר בין משתנים תרבותיים לבין בחירה של אסטרטגיות התערבות בקרב עובדים סוציאליים ערבים*. רמת אביב: אוניברסיטת תל אביב.

זליגמן, צ' (2004). תהליך העדות בטיפול בטראומת גילוי העריות: גילום מחדש ועיבוד הטראומה ביחסי ההעברה וההעברה-הנגדית. בתוך צ' זליגמן וז' סולומון (עורכות), *הסוד ושברו: סוגיות בגילוי עריות* (עמ' 240–256). תל אביב: הקיבוץ המאוחד.

חמיסה, ח' (2011). *התנסותם של תלמידים מקבוצת מיעוט בבית ספר של קבוצת הרוב, כששתי הקבוצות נמצאות בסכסוך עיקש: המקרה הפלסטיני-ישראלי* (חיבור לשם קבלת תואר "דוקטור לפילוסופיה"). אוניברסיטת חיפה, חיפה.

יגנה, נ' (30 ביולי, 2012). מוותרים על ישראל: זינוק במספר הבדואים שלומדים ברשות הפלסטינית. *הארץ*. https://www.haaretz.co.il/news/education/1.1788781

יהל, ח'., ואבו-עג'אג', ע. (2021). שבטיות דת ומדינה בחברה הבדואית בין שימור לשינוי. עדכן אסטרטגי. כתב עת רב תחומי לביטחון לאומי, כרך 24, גיליון 2, עמ' 44- 56.

כרמי, ט' (1994). *שירים: מבחר 1994–1951*. תל אביב: דביר.

לוי, נ', ושביט, י' (2015). כרוניקה של אכזבה: אינטגרציה בין ערבים ליהודים בבית ספר יסודי. *סוציולוגיה ישראלית*, טז(2), עמ' 7–30.

לוי־שטראוס, ק' (1973). *החשיבה הפראית*. מרחביה: ספריית פועלים.

ליבליך, ע' (2010). ממחקר לסיפור ולמחזה: המחקר הנרטיבי בין מדע לאומנות. בתוך ר' תובל־משיח וג' ספקטור־מרזל (עורכות), *מחקר נרטיבי: תאוריה, יצירה ופרשנות* (עמ' 379–429). תל אביב: מאגנס ומכון מופ"ת.

ליבליך, ע' (2017). *קולות: עתי חדש בישראל*. חיפה: פרדס ואוניברסיטת חיפה.

מוסקוביצ'י, ס' (2007). התופעה של ייצוגים חברתיים (תרגום: א' אור). בתוך א' אור וס' בן אשר (עורכות), *המוכר והזר: ייצוגים חברתיים בקבוצות בישראל* (עמ' 19–67). שדה בוקר: אוניברסיטת בן־גוריון בנגב, מכון בן־גוריון לחקר ישראל והציונות.

מכון מאיירס ג'וינט ברוקדייל (2017). *הבדואים בנגב: עובדות ומספרים*. https://brookdale.jdc.org.il/wp-content/uploads/2018/01/MJB-Facts-and_Figures-The-Bedouin-in-the-Negev_2017-05-Hebrew.pdf

נטור, נ' ולוזובסקי, ר' (2010). חובת הדיווח על מקרים של התעללות מינית בילדים – עמדות של יועצים חינוכיים במגזר הערבי. *הייעוץ החינוכי*, 16, עמ' 69–89.

ניג'ם־אכתילאת, פ', בן רבי, ד' וסבו־לאל, ר' (2018). *עקרונות עבודה והתערבות המותאמים לחברה הערבית בשירותי רווחה וטיפול בישראל* (דוח מחקר דמ־778-18). ירושלים: מכון מאיירס־ג'וינט־ברוקדייל, מרכז אנגלברג לילדים ולנוער.

סדן, ע' (2012). מעבר לטראומה והחלמה. *פסיכולוגיה עברית*. https://www.hebpsy.net/articles.asp?id=2714

סיכסק, א' (2016). *תשרין*. תל אביב: אחוזת בית.

ספקטור־בן ארי, ש' (2013א). *הסדרת התיישבות הבדואים בנגב*. ירושלים: הכנסת, מרכז המחקר והמידע.

ספקטור־בן ארי, ש' (2013ב). *פוליגמיה בקרב האוכלוסייה הבדואית בישראל – עדכון*. ירושלים: הכנסת, מרכז המחקר והמידע.

ספקטור־מרזל, ג' (2017). סיפורה של פרשת הקישון כאוטואתנוגרפיה בריקולז'ית. *עיונים בשפה וחברה, 10(1)*, עמ' 214–219.

עבד אלכרים, ע"ר (2015). *חוויותיהם של הורים ערביים בהקשר לחינוך ילדיהם בבתי ספר יהודיים* (עבודת גמר לקבלת תואר "מוסמך בייעוץ חינוכי". המכללה האקדמית לחינוך ע"ש קיי.

עמיחי, י' (2015). המדבר צריך גרפולוג. בתוך א' שחף (עורכת), *שירים על ארץ הנגב*. ישראל: הקיבוץ המאוחד.

פוקו, מ' (1996). *תולדות המיניות: הרצון לדעת*. תל אביב: הקיבוץ המאוחד.

צבר בריהושע, נ' (2016). תפיסות, אסטרטגיות וכלים מתקדמים. בתוך נ' צבר בריהושע (עורכת), *מסורות וזרמים במחקר האיכותני* (עמ' 11–22). תל אביב: מופ"ת.

קדריעובדיה, ש' וקשתי, א' (6 בדצמבר, 2018). האיכות מנצחת את הזהות. *הארץ*. https://www.haaretz.co.il/news/education/.premium-1.6721705

קרק, ר' (2023). *הנגב והבדואים: נוודות, שטחי מחייה וסוגיית הקרקעות, 1800–1967*, Israel Academic Press.

רובין, ש' ויאסין-איסמעיל, ה' (2006). אובדן ושכול בקרב מוסלמים בישראל: קבלת רצון האל, חוויית היגון, והקשר המתמשך לנפטר. *שיחות, כא(1)*, עמ' 44–50.

רובין, ש', מלקינסון, ר' וויצטום, א' (2016). *הפנים הרבות של האובדן והשכול: תיאוריה וטיפול*. חיפה: פרדס.

רודניצקי, א' ואבו ראס, ת' (2011). *החברה הבדואית בנגב*. נווה אילן: יוזמות קרן אברהם.

רודריגז-גארסיא, ח' (2015). *מופעים של ידע: החוויה הפנימית של טהרת המשפחה בקרב נשים דתיות לאומיות מעקבות גיל שונות* (חיבור לשם מילוי חלקי של הדרישות לקבלת תואר "דוקטור לפילוסופיה"). אוניברסיטת בן-גוריון בנגב, באר שבע.

שויד, א', שביט, י', דלאשה, מ', ואופק, מ' (2014). שילוב יהודים וערבים בבתי ספר בישראל (סדרת ניירות מדיניות, נייר מס' 12). בתוך *דוח מצב המדינה – חברה, כלכלה ומדיניות 2014* (עמ' 285–303). ירושלים: מרכז טאוב.

שידלובסקי, א' (2018). עוני נרטיבי ועוני כלכלי. *לקסי-קיי, 9*, 3–5.

שלומי, ט' וציונית, י' (2015). המסע אחר הכבוד האבוד: על רגישות תרבותית בטיפול בילדים שנפגעו מינית בחברה הבדווית (ריאיון עם רוקיה מרזוק אבורקייק). *נקודת מפגש, 9*, עמ' 17–22.

שפירא, ר' (1972). כמו צמח בר. בתוך *ארבע אחר הצהריים* (דיסק 3). רמת השרון: NMC.

www.ingramcontent.com/pod-product-compliance
Lightning Source LLC
Chambersburg PA
CBHW060018100426

42740CB00010B/1513